Planned & Organized Deficit Spending

(PODS)

2nd Edition

By Dr. Vidur Sahgal

Edited by
Ms. Manika Malhotra Jain

IT & Technical Assistant by
Ms. Akanksha Singh

Dr. Vidur Sahgal
Planned & Organized Deficit Spending (PODS)

Published by BooxAI
1500 Getaway Blvd, Boynton Beach, FL
ISBN: 979-8-89383–056-9

Dedicated to my Dad Mr. Tilak Raj Sahgal & my Mum, Mrs. Asha Sahgal.

Thanks & love to my immediate and extended family, as well as thanks to all my friends, peers, and associates.

Also, dedicated to all those lonely people who searched & achieved their dreams alone, however long it took & overcame whatever crossed their paths to achieve them. Believe in yourselves & well done!

Preface

This is the first time that “Planned & Organized” has been added to the words “Deficit Spending”. Modern Monetary Theory (Mitchell et.al 2019), a comparable alternative, originally sourced to Australian economist Bill Mitchell, and developed further by him, Warren Mosler & L. Randall Wray way back, as claimed in 1992, & Professor Stephanie Kelton’s book published in June 2020 called “The Deficit Myth” (Kelton., 2019), came close to realizing PODS, but the major difference between PODS & MMT was that MMT still believed in taxes whereas PODS does not. The subject of Economics has its head underground amidst sophisticated math & statistical methods and analysis, that give the impression, like too an ostrich, that everything is going well mathematically with one’s head underground, but not at ground level. Every time someone blames the subject, math becomes even more complicated and sophisticated while serving no real purpose. To prove PODS theory, there is no need for rigorous mathematics, but rather, economists should understand the logic of PODS by Liabilities of issued E-Digital Cash are balanced with Assets made from this E Digital- cash!! Maybe after reading PODS, the math and statistical analysis, along with other econometric and regression analysis tools will be able to manage economics as a subject where we all, as economists, settle the entire world. It is no longer “Economics” or home accounts & finances, it is “Arthshastra” - the meaning of an economic or commercial decision, at any given moment, based on mutually acceptable exchange. PODS is indebted in its formation to the conceptualization of "Deficit Spending" (Keynes et.al 2015) by Professor John Maynard Keynes, who suggested that deficit spending was a necessary tool required to pull out various affected economies after the Great Depression of 1929 and thereafter. Here what I want to write about, is my understanding of the two words "Deficit Spending" which Professor John coined, in an uncluttered understanding, and not by the mathematical and statistical analysis, meaning(s) and evolution of its rules, processes, and procedures added by Professor Keynes himself, or by his followers. It is to be noted that deficit spending is prevalent in most countries even currently, but with too much international red tape, which is not letting it bloom to its real potential as PODS. "Planned & Organized" today are more important words than Deficit Spending and taken together as PODS provide the magic in economics to sustainably give the world hope and satisfactory futures for all. Distributed Equilibrium Allowable Deficit Spending theory (DEADS) has evolved from Organized & Planned Deficit Spending (OPDS) to Planned & Organized Deficit Spending (PODS), which suggests that deficit spending can be planned and organized in a manner such that it potentially eliminates the need for taxes and minimizes capital shortages and market fluctuations (inflation or deflation). I am tempted to make it preplanned instead of Planned. This book is a culmination of 37 years of thought, discussions, and reading articles in newspapers and magazines whose articles mapped the progress of economic activity across the world. During this period, the globe from isolated countries evolved into one global village and it is only recently in the last two to three years that this global village is being pulled apart and divided. PODS strives to fulfil the globe's objectives in climate change and for good not to be determined by which countries win a war being the good people and the rest evil. PODS have inherent qualities to tempt everyone to follow the good path and, if practiced properly, would achieve this ideal environment. There are no egotistical mindsets practicing PODS, and when fully in place it will result in heaven on earth for all. I wish all those who will put in the hard, punctual work all the best and will never underestimate that their work is not trivial and easy to do. It is important to mention that I have stayed away from most economic jargon and have mentioned very few references. This is because most of the theory of PODS (except the deficit spending part which has been venerably referred to Professor John Maynard Keynes) has been out of the box and original. As far as I know, to the best of my knowledge, this is true, and I hope I haven't unknowingly stepped on anyone's toes where originality is concerned. In any case, I appeal & plead to all economists across the world to put their egos and pride aside and research PODS with so much research leads in this book to choose from. Do inform me if any of you conduct research on PODS. I would love to assist and even partake. I apologize for the low quality of my PODS first edition but thank all those who bought the book and went on to read it, even though I received less than USD 9 dollars as payments for sales to my bank account. I would like to solicit all central bankers and chief economic advisors to respect the IPR of PODS if received directly or indirectly via other consultants, and if used in any way at any time, pay for it in the domestic CBDC of the economy that the central bank represents.

Acknowledgments

Besides my acknowledgments of the first edition, I would like to thank my IT Assistant Ms. Akanksha Singh and editor Ms. Manika Malhotra Jain. My source of inspiration, my mother kept me going when the going was rough.

Foreword

"As progress in machine learning, IOT & artificial intelligence advances, do labour, staff & management in relevant industries or sectors, face unemployment? For example, has the keyboard been replaced already & data entry operators & typists have been laid off? Did we evolve from AI enabled robots and machines that overcame coding restraints and bio-chemically configured themselves as humans are today."

Contents

1. Introduction

Planned & Organized Deficit Spending (PODS) is an evolution of the Distributed Equilibrium Allowable Deficit Spending theory (DEADS). It proposes a strategic approach to deficit spending that could potentially eliminate the need for taxes and mitigate capital shortages and market fluctuations, such as inflation or deflation. In contrast to DEADS, where 'allowable' referred to resource availability beyond monetary considerations, PODS places a central focus on the resources produced and available for an economy's population within a given period. The critical goal is to gradually build up a sustainable saturation level of supply for all products, services, and agricultural goods in the economy to all its economic units. Under PODS, the concept of 'saturation' becomes paramount. It suggests that over time, any product introduced into the economy can achieve full and sustainable supply without disruptions, making saturation the ultimate target. An essential aspect of PODS is that it won't lead to the displacement of current personnel. On the contrary, the economic and commerce sectors are expected to require millions of additional personnel, thereby creating more employment opportunities. Moreover, these new roles would demand minimal training in the theory, making the transition relatively smooth and inclusive.

This brief is specific to India, but PODS can be used globally. I've written this with India in mind because I'd preferably like to see our backyard in order, before attempting to put others in order. India still has 900 million people who live in abject poverty. These citizens must be addressed first before we look beyond our international borders. These also present the greatest business/commercial opportunity in the history of the free world. There are approximately 900 million potential consumers/producers waiting to be activated, not to mention the approximately 4-500 million existing consumers/producers, as reported. Populations should be considered as valuable assets within large markets, comprising both manual labour (for example our excess labour can be sent to rebuild Ukraine provided that their war with Russia ends) and knowledge- based contributions besides the brain power which could be harnessed by the individual given the proper knowledge environment. These populations engage in simultaneous production and consumption activities. However, it's important to note that recognizing populations as assets does not imply an endorsement of uncontrolled or unsustainable population growth.

Today: If I, as an economic unit, want to produce something, I need money. If I want to consume something, I need money. If I do not have money, I really am not a producer or a consumer, in the real tangible sense. But if I have access to money, in a controlled and efficient manner, I, as an economic unit, would produce and consume, adding to the bottom line...The GDP, the entire population (1.4 billion) of the economy, could then become an economy of producers & consumers, perfectly coordinated, in such a manner, so as to produce no inflation and at the same time achieve market equilibrium for every pre-identified product(s), agro(s) & service(s). Equilibrium here and hereafter in this book means market saturation or full supply to the market. It does not mean where the demand and supply curves intersect each other. Agro means a vegetable, fruit, and includes horticulture, herbs, and commercial, natural, and agricultural produce forms. A service is an act or use that a consumer, business, or government is willing to pay for. Work done by barbers, doctors, lawyers, mechanics, banks, insurance companies, and others is an example.

In market economics, the goal is to meet the demand for specific products, agriculture, or services by ensuring an optimal combination of quality and pricing. This involves supplying precisely the quantity required and offering the right number of choices for each identified product, agro, or service. Even deflation can be acceptable because it increases real income, even if wages remain constant. It's crucial to recognize that one of the most formidable barriers in this process is money. Money plays a pivotal role as both the means to create and consume goods and services. If an individual lacks the necessary funds to manufacture a TV, they cannot do so. Similarly, if someone wants to purchase a TV but lacks the funds, they are unable to make the purchase. Therefore, the absence of money in an economy can be likened to arthritis in a champion golfer, hindering both production and consumption.

Do note, however, that one does not have to produce, but must consume. This is how nature made us. And as a natural consumer, arguably the state should provide a good standard of easy access to the basics at least, with luxuries and desires being met by economic activity, also provided by the state. For example, food can be given free at a state restaurant, but if one wants to buy a TV, then one would have to work to earn/ buy the TV... or work at a TV manufacturing factory.

In the framework of Planned & Organized Deficit Spending (PODS), digital money is strategically channeled into the Demand (I prefer calling Demand: Request.) and Supply "Pipelines". The government administrators overseeing PODS ensure that for each pre-identified product, agricultural item, or service, one unit or more of money injected into the Demand channel corresponding to the production of one unit or more of actual physical Supply. This demand-supply match must be physically made for each pre-identified product, agro, or service to maintain market equilibrium and work towards achieving sustainable saturation. Assuming the Demand/Supply lag away, the number of monies distributed for a match by actual physical supply, or production of pre-identified products or services, can be magnified many times over, if such Demand Supply matches continue all the way to market equilibrium, and eventually full saturation/supply for the demand of any pre-identified product, agro or service. This assumption of assuming the supply/demand lag is important, in that for example, if the government of this economy was to decide that every economic unit should be able to buy a TV (now a state/government pre-identified desirable product for every economic unit), and assuming the sum of economic unit is 1.4 billion people, then it would take time to set up the production capabilities to manufacture 1.4 billion TVs. At the same time, it would also take time to provide employment to the economic unit (One person in this case) so they can earn enough through various local currency economic activities, possibly including government jobs, to afford their desired TV.

PODS is theoretically robust and highly practical, requiring only minor adjustments, adjustments in the current economic structure, to bring it into existence.

The broad skeletal framework of PODS is as follows:

The described economy, under the control of a central organization, manages its currency through electronic digital money issuance. The government acts as the custodian and distributor of these funds and their electronic transactions. It's essential to emphasize that these funds originate solely from the non-animate E-digital electronic platform, which possesses the capability to print and issue both paper and digital currency. This platform is created and operated by the government solely for economic purposes. It should be clear from the beginning that these capitals/monies are not government-owned but public-owned. The government comes and goes, but it is the public that decides the government, at least in what is supposedly Democratic India. The amounts of money that are available from this Digital Mint (DM) are infinite and are a function of how much the government in charge is willing to spend: spend in a planned or organized manner, the manner of which is explained later. It is to be noted that Modern Monetary Systems are totally electronic with electronic digital credits and debits operating from one's cell phone to each other's (as an example). So, you can pay electro digitally from your own cell phone to the bookstore owner's cell phone and pay for this book.

Do note here, that the government, can, in this case, pay itself amounts that could usher in a Zero Corruption form of governance. The Government can pay its Bureaucracy, Public Sector Government Companies, Organizations & Departments. Not to forget the politicians also. One of the reasons corruptions exists is an inherent bottleneck in the relevant economy. You will note that surplus economies tend to have no or very little corruption, while shortage economies have corruption.

1. 50 Desirables/Necessities, 200 Economic Units/People: In this scenario, there is an insufficient supply of 50 desirables/necessities to meet the demands of 200 economic units/people. This situation creates intense competition for these limited resources, which can lead to corrupt practices as individuals or entities try to gain an advantage or secure a share of these resources. Corruption often arises from the imbalance between supply and demand, where those with more resources or influence may gain an unfair advantage.
2. 50 Desirables/Necessities, 40 Economic Units/People: In contrast, when there are only 50 desirables/necessities but a smaller population of 40 economic units/people, the situation is different. There is a sufficient supply to meet the needs of all economic units, with 10 resources left over. In this case, there is no incentive for corruption as everyone can access what they need without competing or resorting to unethical practices. Additionally, the surplus of 10 desirables/necessities can be potentially exported to benefit the economy further.

To eradicate corruption in economies, addressing supply and demand bottlenecks for essential goods and services is vital. Additionally, surplus economies engaging in corruption should face international isolation and be labelled as rogue states by the global community.

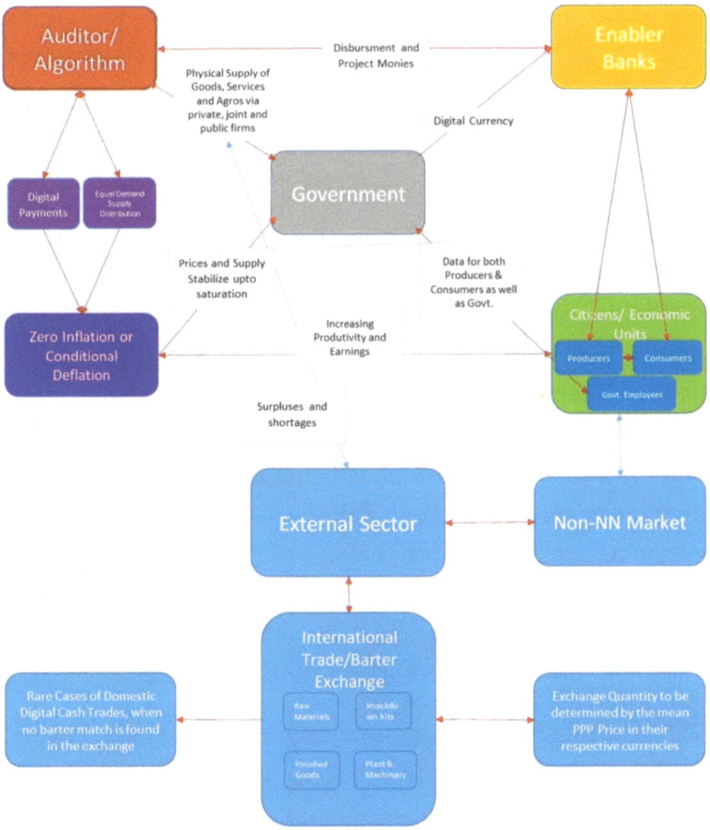

Accordingly, the initial formula for PODS is explained in Box 1. PODS FLOWCHART:

Figure 1: PODS Flow Chart

Explanation: The Government instructs and issues digital currency through the Enabler Banks which supply this to the producers and consumers as per PODS Rules & Regulations. At the same time, the auditors are informed, who see to it that digital payments to personnel are made and ensure that equal demand and supply distribution takes place, while economic activity data of the Citizens/Economics Units, who act as producers, consumers as well as government employees, are brought to the government's notice such that there is no inflation or deflation. Hence, prices stabilize, and the next round of demand supply equilibrium is started by the Government up to aggregate demand and supply being saturated.

External Sector: Whatever Surpluses or Shortages are experienced in the domestic economy, will be directed to the International Barter Exchange. This provides barter for raw materials, knockdown kits, finished goods, and plant & machinery which can be used to manufacture finished goods; with the exchange transactions being determined by looking at each transacting country's PPP exchange prices. Any trade not facing closure in the IBE can be conducted in the digital currencies of the participating economies. In case of surpluses cannot be absorbed by the IBE, can be reintroduced into the domestic producer non NN market.

The government, to start applying PODS, would have to identify an economic unit (be it an individual or a family) and thereafter pre-identify a basket of products & services which every economic unit should enjoy, so as to supply the same to the economic unit. After that, the entire economy consisting of the sum of its economic units would build up to producing and consuming the pre-identified basket of products and services. In this manner, the government would know beforehand, what it needs to produce and what will be consumed and will accordingly provide (also, if required, digitally issue) the monies required to execute this/this economic activity(ies). One would also have to look at the resources available, but domestic monies will not be a constraint for acquiring adequate resources.

During the transition from the current macro & micro-economic system to the PODS system, there will be a set of financial measures implemented:

1. All economic units will be required to deposit their money into the banks during this transition, with no questions asked. This money will be shredded and burnt so that it cannot be deposited twice.
2. A fixed, tax-free interest rate of 11 percent, calculated on simple interest basis, will be applied to these legitimate cash deposits. This encourages citizens to participate in the transition and ensure they receive a reasonable return on their deposits.
3. Individuals who pay taxes, especially those who are living together with immediate family, will be paid with a 11 % simple interest rate on the total tax amounts paid up to transition date. Additionally, the total tax paid by the assesses economic unit will be deposited as capital in their digital bank account.

No global market for any product or service to date has even been close to achieving "equilibrium". Or there is no market for any product, agro, or service that has been fully sustainably supplied globally. There have been small & medium (in terms of population) developed economies that have achieved some level of market equilibrium in Natural Needs (NN), a grim situation but a real situation.

Now, let's shift focus to understand the basic theory of marketing with the objective of attaining full sustainable, saturated supply (SSS) for products/services categorized as "natural needs" (NN). In my opinion, the following list comprises the needs of an individual family economic units which all governments should provide in a supervised manner:

1. Nutritious Carbon Free Cooked Food.
2. Clothes.
3. Clean water covering all human usage requirements.
4. Shelter.
5. Education: Students from the start should be paid well to study. Studies should be equated to a paid job, irrespective of the level of study.
6. Health.
7. Judiciary & Police.
8. Carbon-free transport.
9. Connectivity.
10. Supervised & Incentivized Old age care by the family members of senior citizens.
11. A clean environment.
12. One solar-powered light, cooler, and computer point charger.
13. One smartphone and one laptop along with a solar charger for each.
14. Electronic banking for all either online or via cell phone.

There would be an Economic Administrative Committee (EAC), that would decide on choices and brands of the NN's and at the same time would decide what luxuries and desirables/wants will be allowed to citizens who work to earn over and above their supervised allowed limits.

Note: that the above welfare sectors are prevalent in many countries, some of which are developed very well. So, these areas don't need endorsements from other economies or the IMF, etc. All they require are smart economists and politicians who are generous enough to spend on their subjects while having the PODS model rock solid behind them.

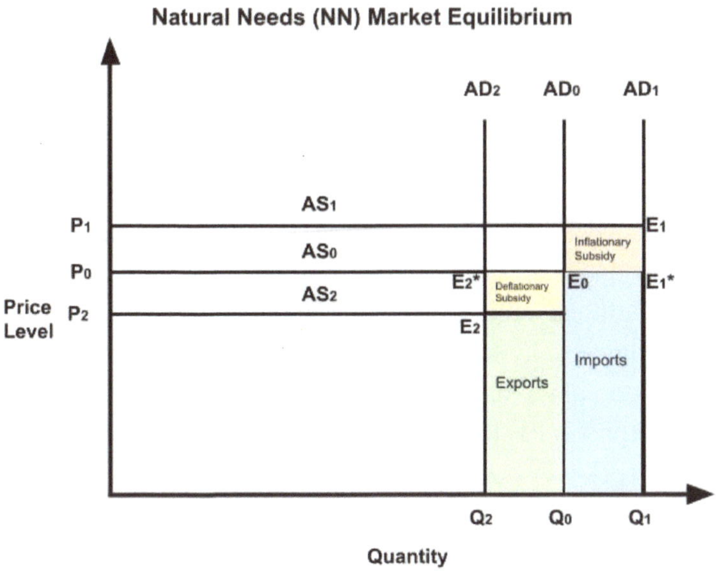

Figure 2: Natural Needs (NN) Market Equilibrium

To explain the NN world via graphs:

Imports = (Q1-Q0), Value of Imports = P1* (Q1-Q0), Subsidy = (P1-P0)*(Q1-Q0) = **Additional Cost of Imports, Exports = (Q0-Q2), Value of Exports = P0*(Q0-Q2)**

The AS Curve: The Aggregate Supply curve is horizontal because the government procures the NN goods at a fixed price. Hence, Supply is perfectly Elastic.

The AD Curve: The Aggregate Demand curve is vertical because the demand is fixed and given. It is a function of population and the number of units allowed per citizen per product or service.

The Equilibrium Mechanism:

1. **Excess Demand:** The Initial Demand-Supply Equilibrium is observed at E0. If the aggregate demand shifts to the right (mostly because of increasing population), we see that the new demanded quantity shifts from Q0 to Q1. Now, this additional required supply cannot be bridged domestically leading to a need of imports from the external sector- (inflationary effects). If the cost of import is P1, the new equilibrium level is attained at E1. However, the cost difference between the domestic and the external sector (P1-P0) is subsidized by the government to nullify the imported items' inflationary effect (being of a higher imported price), which brings the equilibrium to E1*. Hence, Price levels remain unchanged at P0.
2. **Low Demand:** When the aggregate demand shifts to the left (mostly due to people wilfully opting out of the NN Market and migrating to the non-NN Market, as well as oversupply of production), the demand drops to Q2 from Q0. -Consequently, there is excess supply of the NN goods, which can be exported to the external sector, at a potentially lower price P2 -The Domestic Equilibrium shifts to E2* and the quantity Q2-Q0 is exported at P0 after a deflationary subsidy of (P0-P2) is given to the exporter. Hence, the prices again remain unchanged at a zero-state P0.

Figure 3: Resources Vs Supply

Increased Supply (due to more resources being available) Deflationary Subsidy, assuming constant demand (T1 to T2). Decreased Supply (due to fewer resources being available) Inflationary Subsidy assuming constant demand (T4 to T5).

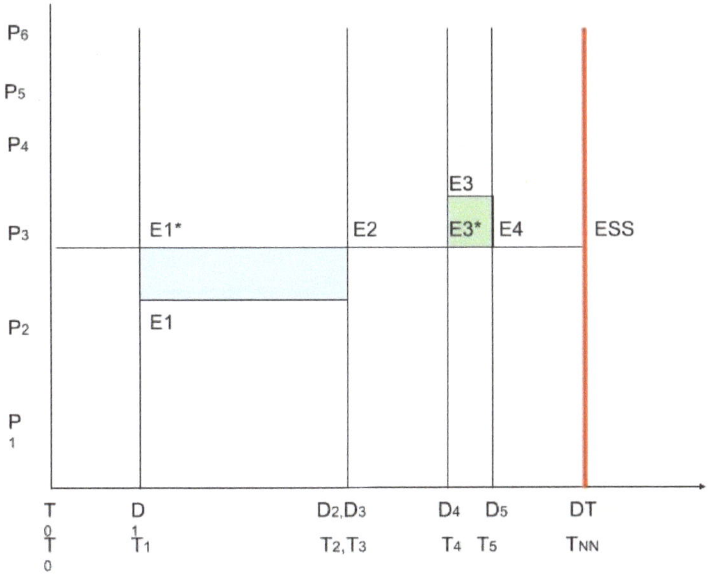

Figure 4: Dynamic interplay between supply, demand, and available resources over time

Explanation: In the given scenario, a dynamic interplay between supply, demand, and available resources over time is described, resulting in deflationary and inflationary effects on prices, which the government manages through subsidies. At T0, there is zero demand and supply. At T1, there is normal demand and supply and available resources with an equilibrium price being constant throughout as in above graph.

At T2, available resources double in quantity and impact a deflationary effect on prices, assuming normal demand and increased Supply (due to more resources being available). Deflationary Subsidy, assuming constant demand where from E1, we move to E1* to achieve a zero state, and D2 and D3 get supplied and consumed at T2 and T3. This Deflationary effect is the shaded blue portion in figure 2. Similarly, at T4 and T5, there were less resources available and the period also, as noted T4 and T5, created an inflationary effect on prices and the government gave an inflation subsidy to bring the prices back to Zero state, as indicated by the area shaded in the green region in the above graph. This normal and abnormal supply continues all the way up to sustainable saturation supply.

2. Pods Initial Formulae

Box 1

INITIAL FORMULAE OF PODS:

1. $\sum$(R)= $\sum$(S)= $\sum$(D)” either from P/J or G sectors with "I" (Inflation) = Zero as the target.
>> where
>> “R” = All requests of a product/service of all citizens, or economic units of an economy
>> “S” = Supply of the product/service
>> “D” = Demanded Quantity
>> “I” = Inflation
>> P=Private, J=Joint, G=Government.

Cft (consumers frequency in the subject time-period) in Pre-determined Time (PDT) of products, goods, services & agros = $\sum$(D) or $\sum$(R)

+

Pft (producers’ frequency in subject time-period) in PDT is

equal to CFT, if negligible non-affecting time lag between D & S or R to prevent Inflation of Deflation in product prices (ranging from 1 to infinity)

The relationship between these variables can be summarized as follows:

$\sum(D/R) + \sum(S)$= Gross Deficit Products, services, goods & agros ($\sum$=1,2,3,4…., ∞)

Or Aggregate Demand (($\sum(D/R)$) is a sum of Cft in a Pdt, as an economic unit consume and produce

Where Cft = consumption-frequency per time-period or demand per economic unit &

Where Pft = production of goods, services, products & agros matching the Cft D or R as per above.

$\sum(D/R)$ = Total Aggregate Demand/Request $\sum$(Supply), resulting in Gross Deficit Product (GDP), where Total S supports Total D/R $\sum(D/R)$ =Total Aggregate Demand/Request and eventually equals (with passage of non-inflationary or deflationary time) = $\sum$(Supply) = Gross Deficit Product (GDP) where Total S supports Total D/R

So, what is produced in an economy supports that country's currency.

Domestic Money availability in the economy is infinite subject to resources or factors of production.

Y= consumption= production (no stocks) Y= NN + NNN

NN= w.Y

AD (Aggregate Demand) in NN= Population * $\sum$Xi (where i =1,2,3…….,14) GDP = C + I + G+ (X-M)

C= c.Y

I= b-iR

3. Market Economics/Mix And Additional Analysis

The 8Ps of The Marketing Mix

Traditionally, we've been taught about the "4 P's" of Marketing, and over time, this framework has expanded to encompass the 7 Ps. To recap, these 7 Ps are:

1. Product
2. Price
3. Place
4. Promotion
5. People
6. Positioning
7. Processes
8. Performances

However, an essential element seems to have been overlooked in this framework, and it's the "Providing" of monies (9th). This can be seen as the very first and most critical "P" as it ensures that both producers and consumers have the means to engage in economic activities related to the product or service being marketed and 10th P being PURR (Product Usage Responsibility Regulation).

The Importance of Money as a Given

Money is widely accepted as a fundamental aspect of modern economies. It's considered a given, and its presence has enabled many countries to navigate challenging situations like the Covid-19 pandemic by providing stimulus packages without resorting to significant tax increases.

Transforming Tender Systems

In the realm of tender systems, there's a shift needed. Currently, tenders often focus solely on choosing the "Cheapest-L1" option, with less consideration for other critical factors. This approach is flawed as it often disregards the importance of quality and overall value. The L1 system never gets completed on time and the vendor keeps blackmailing GoI for more money to complete the project having met the budget with L1.

The new approach should transition from "The Cheapest-L1" to "The Best/Optimum-O1." This means considering not just the cost but also the tangible and intangible benefits and costs associated with any project or initiative.

To ensure transparency and efficiency, every tender submission should include a Critical Path Method (CPM) and Matching Decision Tree Analysis in Real-Time Reports. By doing so, we can make more informed decisions regarding cost and revenue, accounting for both quantitative and qualitative aspects.

The Role of Government in Monetary Control

The government holds a unique role as the sole custodian and distributor of electronic digital monies. Unlike traditional taxation, it has the capacity to generate funds without imposing any tax burdens on the public. This financial independence allows the government to operate more flexibly and efficiently in managing economic resources, providing stimulus when necessary, and maintaining financial stability.

4. Pods - No Taxes, Why?

Taxes have historically been associated with monarchies and are incongruous with the principles of true democracies and capitalist economies. In a democratic and capitalist society, taxes that are not voluntary contradict the foundational ideals of these systems. Monarchs historically levied taxes for purposes like defense or aggression, which are no longer relevant in today's world, where peaceful coexistence and economic cooperation among nations take precedence.

Taxes often carry a demotivating factor and can hinder individual and economic growth. While philanthropic or voluntary contributions to public spending are a different matter, mandatory taxes can stifle individual initiative. If taxes were eliminated and replaced with voluntary contributions, people might feel more inspired to work for themselves, and governments would no longer be burdened with justifying their spending to taxpayers.

It's worth noting that in a state with a highly sought-after international currency, the government could expedite supply by importing goods like TVs. In a welfare state, such items might even be distributed free of charge to citizens.

Another stated purpose of taxes by experts is to achieve equitable wealth distribution. However, when the government controls THE E-DIGITAL MINT, it can efficiently and equitably distribute wealth without relying on campaign donations from business interests. Since there are no taxes, the government is not accountable for revenue collection but can focus on enabling producers and consumers. In this system, government spending can be evaluated by citizens during elections, providing transparency and accountability without the need for taxation.

In India, there exists a parallel economy known as the Black Money Economy, which operates alongside the formal, or "white," economy. The distinction between which of these two economies is larger is not the primary focus. Instead, within the framework of Planned & Organized Deficit Spending (PODS), these two economies are considered to be of approximately equal size, estimated to amount to a combined value of around six trillion dollars.

The absence of Planned & Organized Deficit Spending (PODS) can be seen as a contributing factor to the issues faced in the example mentioned. In a system where PODS is practiced, individuals like Lala ji would have the opportunity to earn a fair and legal interest on their capital of INR 10 million at a rate of 11% per annum, all tax-free. This would motivate them to use digital transactions through their local banks without the fear of tax authorities identifying their undisclosed income and subsequently confiscating their money. All people who have paid legal taxes, their paid taxes will be added during the entire tenure of the payment adjusted for inflation and a deposit will be made in each past taxy payees account with a 13%-18% interest per annum all 100% guarantee.

In a PODS system, all cash currency monies will be invited into Banks, no questions asked and deposited amount would be credited to their accounts with a 100% guarantee of the deposit amount and 11% interest per annum to motivate them not to speculate. The cash deposited will be burnt so that it may not be deposited again. The three Rules of such banking are:

1. You can only transact digitally
2. You cannot speculate with your interest earning or capital
3. You cannot encash your deposits in any currency

By implementing PODS, individuals like Lala ji would be incentivized to bring their financial activities into the formal economy, resulting in greater transparency and legal compliance. It would also eliminate the need for parallel, informal economic transactions that contribute to price distortions.

In this scenario, the logistics cost associated with transporting, packaging, branding, and processing the rice from the grower farmer's village to other locations would be the primary cost justified in the eventual price paid by the consumer. This would lead to a more efficient and equitable economic system, benefiting both individuals and the overall economy.

5. How To Equate Demand And Supply In Monetary Units?

Equating demand and supply In the PODS framework, the equilibrium between supply and demand is uniquely orchestrated. It all starts with a specific commodity, denoted as C1, whose unit of supply is equated to the digital money required for consumers to purchase it at the Maximum Retail Price (MRP). This forms the basis of pricing, ensuring that money supplied in the demand channel remains as income, while money in the supply channel converts into tangible goods, services, or agricultural products. The value of the domestic currency in a PODS economy is inherently linked to the commodities it enables the supply of, rather than being tied to foreign currencies or precious metals. Through this equilibrium, the system establishes consistent pricing across the country. Furthermore, PODS introduces a subsidy mechanism to support consumers when market prices exceed the Minimum Support Price (MSP) and producers when prices fall below it. This approach has the potential for global application, offering a structured and dynamic way to balance supply and demand while ensuring economic stability.

One unit of supply of C1= x units of digital money at MRP cost of demand = one unit of supply MRP, because Producer's Price, Packing, Processing, Branding, and Logistics (PPBC) and logistics cost is averaged and equal at each farmgate or factory gate. This way, the Price level can be constant across the country.

So, we conclude, supply unit of physical goods, service or agro is required for C1 – and its MSP + PPBC = MRP = x digital units of money arrived at C1 onwards, of the demand unit which will equate with the supply unit.

Therefore, one unit of supply will be equal to its corresponding unit of demand where both supply and demand start off as money, but the supply ends up as goods, service or agro (Cost of the commodity C1 and its MSP need not be the same).

If $P^1n > MSP$ = then consumers will be subsidized If $P^1n < MSP$ = then producers will be subsidized (P^1n is the price in the respective countries for the respective product).

$$MSP\ of\ C = \frac{P1c + P2c + P3c + \cdots Pnc}{\Sigma n}$$

Where 1,2, 3…,n denotes countries.

Supply is complete when quantity demand is produced, and consumer products match each other and are physically consumed. These would be easy to calculate actual supply demand physical production & consumption, but where services are concerned, one would need to calculate service supply & physical consumption with as much precision as possible.

6. Pricing Value (S)

In the current retail pricing system, the Maximum Retail Price (MRP) is determined by adding various components, including the Minimum Support Price (MSP), the margins of numerous brokerages or commissions, processing, packaging, branding, and logistics costs. Unfortunately, in this system, farmers typically receive only 20% of the MRP, shopkeepers get 11%, and the remaining 69% is distributed among the various intermediaries involved in the supply chain.

The key question is how to arrive at the MSP. Under the PODS framework, MSP calculation follows a scientific and inflation-free approach. Here's how it works:

To determine the MSP for a product like Apples in India, a global analysis is conducted by aggregating the MSP Purchasing Power Parity Prices (PPPP) for Apples from all member countries of the Food and Agriculture Organization (FAO). The average mean PPPP is calculated, and this price, when converted to the domestic currency, becomes the MSP that farmers will receive at their village or farmgate in India.

This standardized price serves as the reference point for the farmer.

Moreover, major retailers like Walmart would adopt a consistent MSP for Apples across all their store locations, aligning with the average value derived from the global PPPP analysis. It's important to note that while farmgate prices and other costs like processing, packaging, and branding may be uniform globally based on PPPP, logistics costs can vary depending on the distance from the farmgate or store to the actual consumer.

Using a similar methodology, PPPP values can be calculated for all items listed in the Wholesale Price Index (WPI), including those in the fuel and power category, and the manufactured products category. This approach ensures that MSP calculations are grounded in a comprehensive, scientifically driven, and inflation-neutral process, providing a fair and stable pricing mechanism.

In the context of PODS (Planned & Organized Deficit Spending), the Law of One Price (LOOP) as articulated by Gustav Cassel encounters significant challenges that make it impractical for several reasons:

1. Historical Development: While the theory of Purchasing Power Parity (PPP), which underlies the LOOP, has its roots dating back to the 16th century, it was further developed and refined by Gustav Cassel in the early 20th century. However, despite its long history, there is still no consensus on PPP theory based on foreign exchange rates. Moreover, international trade continues to be dominated by a few major currencies that are not freely available. Many countries express dissatisfaction with this currency monopoly and seek alternatives.

2. Lack of Uniform Exchange Rates: The absence of a uniform, 1:1 unitary foreign exchange rate across the globe is a significant obstacle to the application of LOOP. Differing exchange rates between currencies hinder the achievement of price parity.
3. Price Variability: Even when considering prices at the source (ex-factory or ex-farm), various factors contribute to price differences between economies. Packaging, processing, and branding costs may remain consistent, but logistical costs are influenced by the distance between the production facility and the consumer market. These logistical variations impact on the final price.
4. Regional Mark-ups: Trade and broker profit margins, which play a role in determining prices, can vary widely from one factory or farm to another within each economy. As a result, uniform pricing across regions becomes challenging due to these varying mark-ups.

Given these practical challenges and the complex nature of international trade, achieving price parity according to the traditional Law of One Price remains elusive. PODS acknowledges these realities and seeks to establish a pricing mechanism that is grounded in scientific principles and considers the intricacies of real-world economics.

The objective of PODS is to establish a universal pricing system for standardized items, such as specific quality grades of products or identical models of consumer goods, across all countries in the world. This system aims to facilitate each country's ability to issue its own currency in a manner that sustains equilibrium between aggregate demand and supply, resulting in zero inflation or deflation—a state of economic stability.

To calculate these average prices, a reference point is determined, known as the Minimum Support Price (MSP), which equates to the wholesale price. Processing, packaging, and branding costs (PPBC) are then added to this MSP. Notably, both the MSP and PPBC will be uniform across all factories and farm gates, ensuring consistency.

The one potential source of price variation between countries lies in logistic costs, which can differ due to varying distances between production facilities and consumer hubs. These logistics costs can be averaged and, if necessary, subsidized to arrive at a standard cost figure applicable to all goods, services, and agricultural products.

Consequently, the primary difference in prices (Maximum Retail Price or MRP) between countries will be attributed to logistics expenses. However, within each economy, the MRP will be uniform across geographic locations. It's important to emphasize the importance of "buying local" to minimize logistical price variations. Practicing this principle allows consumers to benefit from lower prices while retail outlets can realize savings in logistics costs.

In summary, the formula for calculating MRP within the PODS framework is:

MRP = (MSP + PPBC) - Logistic cost

This approach seeks to establish a globally consistent pricing mechanism, fostering economic stability and equitable pricing for standardized items across economies.

In the PODS system, the distribution of costs is as follows:

1. Logistic Cost: The logistic cost is incurred in the transportation and delivery of goods from factories

or farm gates to consumer hubs. It can be managed in two ways. Firstly, it can be a nationally equal charge, meaning that it is standardized and consistent across the entire country, regardless of the distance goods need to travel. Secondly, for longer distances or extra charges associated with shorter distances, the logistic cost can be subsidized. This means that the government, as the provider of Natural Needs (NN) goods, would bear the cost of logistics. The objective is to ensure that overall costs are averaged out and remain affordable for consumers.

2. MRP Cost: The Maximum Retail Price (MRP) represents the final price at which consumers purchase goods. This cost is paid by consumers to retailers. In the PODS system, this cost will be borne primarily by government job incomes. Both government jobs and private jobs will contribute to individuals' incomes, allowing them to afford MRP prices for NN (Natural Needs) goods. Additionally, the government may provide in-kind support for purchasing NN goods or NNN (Non-Natural Needs) goods, giving economic units the flexibility to choose between the two economies based on their preferences and needs.

In summary, the government plays a pivotal role in ensuring that logistics costs remain manageable through subsidies and that individuals can afford MRP prices for NN goods through various income sources, including government jobs and in-kind support.

Flow of Subsidies:

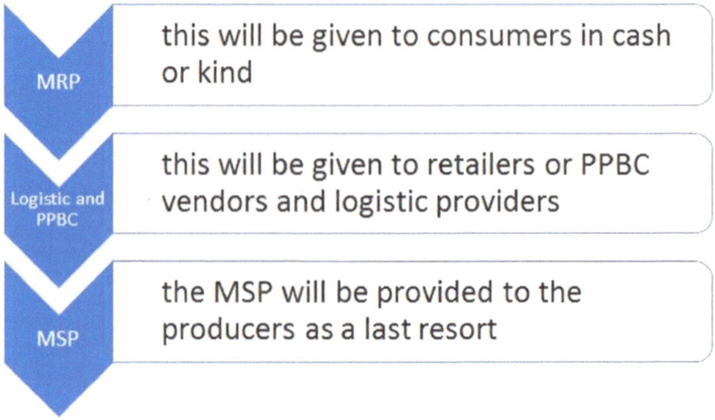

Figure 5: Flow of Subsidies

In the PODS framework, achieving a globally consistent Purchasing Power Parity Price (PPPP) across all countries would be a significant step towards realizing the Law of One Price (LOOP). However, it's important to note that MSPs (Minimum Support Prices) for various items are intended as guiding and support prices. They provide a reference point for producers, farmers, and service providers, ensuring that they are not compelled to sell their products or services at unreasonably low prices. These MSPs serve as a cushion, helping producers make informed price decisions while accounting for seasonality in agricultural produce pricing. If there are no takers for products sold at MSP as a last resort, then these products could be put for sale on the IBE.

In the case of agricultural products, a National Agricultural Produce Government Company (further details to be provided later) will be responsible for purchasing produce directly at the farm gate or village gate, offering digital currency as payment. This ensures that farmers have a secure and fair option for selling their goods. However, farmers or villages are free to explore other selling options voluntarily, even if they choose to sell at different price levels.

Under this system, importing economies have the flexibility to either subsidize imported goods to align their prices with the globally averaged PPPP or impose import taxes if prices are too low compared to the prevailing PPPP. This approach helps maintain price stability and fairness in international trade.

Moreover, it suggests that major currencies should transition towards using PPPP as the basis for foreign exchange rates (FX). This would require realigning FX rates to correspond with derived PPPP values. International banks, including institutions like the World Bank, ICICI Bank Limited, or Punjab National Bank, should adapt their banking systems to accommodate the principles and practices of this paradigm. Further details on this banking paradigm will be provided.

This system aims to establish global price consistency through PPPP, ensuring fair pricing for goods and services while suggesting a transition in major currencies and international banking practices to align with the framework.

7. Money As A Given - Pods Banking Algorithm & Paradigm

To facilitate the transition from the current economic state (referred to as "The Grey") to the envisioned sustainable and green economic model (referred to as "The Green"), the establishment of an Indian Global Bank (IGB) is proposed. Unlike international financial institutions like the IMF, World Bank, and ADB, the IGB will be specifically created to fund and support this transformation. The key features of the IGB and its role in the proposed PODS are as follows:

1. Purpose of the IGB: The primary purpose of the IGB is to provide the necessary funding for economies to transition from The Grey to The Green. This transition will be funded using India's own digital E-currency.
2. Funding Mechanism: Each participating economy in the PODS framework will have the ability to fund its own transition requirements. This can be achieved through currency deficits and bridge currency loans, which may involve the use of

another relevant economy's currency or currencies for purchase of goods and services required for the green economy which will be required in the short run while capacities are shored up to build capacities for these goods and services. These funds will be instrumental in adopting new technologies and expediting the transition process.

3. Non-Profit Orientation: The IGB will operate on a non-profit basis, with its primary objective being the successful transition to a 100% Green economy. It will not focus on generating profits. Instead, the emphasis will be on achieving the desired Green economic state.
4. Analysis and Future Actions: Once the Green is fully realized and implemented, ongoing analysis of the experience gained will guide future actions. The IGB will assess the impact of The Green economy and determine further steps as necessary to ensure sustainability.
5. Digital Currency Implementation: Indian public sector bank branches overseas may be authorized to issue digital Indian E-currency. However, this issuance should be directed exclusively toward Indian businesses, ensuring that payment receipts are conducted using digital Indian E-currency. The IGB will oversee and regulate this process.
6. Export of Qualified Manpower: To support the transition, qualified manpower may be exported. However, these individuals will need to fulfill domestic project requirements or participate in training programs to prepare an adequate workforce for export. This approach ensures that the domestic workforce remains a priority.

Bubble of value

The banking model within the PODS is distinct from traditional banking. It focuses on fostering long-term sustainable production rather than being a typical venture capitalist or angel investor. Key features of this banking model are:

1. Long-Term Commitment: The bank's primary goal is to support and nurture projects for the long run. There is no exit strategy, and instead of exits, entrepreneurs are incentivized with production-linked incentives (PLIs). These PLIs can include credits against the loans issued, reducing the entrepreneur's liability to the bank.
2. Non-Inflationary or Deflationary Rewards: Entrepreneurs have the flexibility to motivate themselves or their colleagues by drawing from the gross profits generated by their projects. These incentives are designed to avoid contributing to inflation or deflation.
3. Zero Interest Loans: The bank offers loans at zero interest rates, available to both domestic and foreign companies setting up operations in India. Production Linked Incentives (PLIs) may be granted, subject to meeting predetermined targets related to quality, quantity, and employment (QQE). Loans and advances are entirely digital, and repayment is also conducted digitally, potentially including any earned PLIs.
4. Strict Accountability: The banking system is committed to maintaining strict accountability. Engaging in banking crimes or failing to meet QQE targets is taken seriously. Firms falling behind in

QQE targets may face probation, and new entrepreneurs could replace original promoters if necessary.

5. Eliminating the Need for Savings: PODS envisions a system where individuals don't need traditional savings. All lifetime milestone expenditures can be covered by zero-percent EMI loans, which can be repaid after enjoying any PLIs or other loan benefits.
6. Full Integration of Responsibilities: Banking in the public sector means that bankers are considered part of the government. They are responsible for providing capital, working capital, and ensuring the realization of retail prices for the products, services, or agricultural produce being supported.

In the PODS Economy, banks will play a pivotal role, serving as the largest employers and facilitating economic activities through planned and organized deficit spending. These banks will employ a wide range of experts, including data entry officers, auditors, supply-side and demand- side monitors, economic coordinators, and traditional banking personnel. Banking operations will run 24/7, with a strong emphasis on delivering supply-side support and crediting loans and advances through Production Linked Incentives (PLIs).

Moving to banking, the traditional concept of paper-based transactions with cheque books and passbooks will be replaced by digital electronic solutions, such as providing high-quality smartphones to account holders. Banks will be responsible for training account holders in using these digital services, ensuring 100% accurate data entry, and maintaining robust cybersecurity measures. Customer support services will be readily available, with zero waiting times, leading to increased job opportunities.

The quality and infrastructure of bank branches will meet specific standards, like those of established institutions like ICICI Bank Ltd. The focus will be on keeping banking fully in the public sector, discouraging private banking, and encouraging partnerships between foreign banks and Indian public sector banks to enable trade in INR.

In the PODS Economy, banks will support physical production and consumption, utilizing data and planning to allocate resources efficiently. Loans for both production and consumption will be interest-free, reducing costs for both producers and consumers and promoting economic growth and sustainability.

The current state of banking sadly, both globally and in India, often adds unnecessary costs to monetary transactions. For instance, the London Interbank Offer Rate (LIBOR), which served as a reference point for short-term interest rates, was used to price various financial products. However, it raises questions when banks take deposits at higher interest rates than LIBOR, as it can increase the cost of borrowing for both banks and customers. In India, the Reserve Bank of India's Repo Rate is relatively low at 6.5%, but banks often offer deposit rates of 6-7%, which may not align with sound banking principles.

If we were to add up all the NPAs, loan write offs, welfare, subsidies, illegal overseas remittances and bankruptcies then may be PODS would be a better banking paradigm then the current global banking system.

In the PODS system, the lending rate of banks would be set at zero, while interest payable on Bonafide deposits would be 11% per annum, tax-free. The cost of running the bank and servicing these loans and deposits would constitute the allowable "deficit" or "cost." This deficit or cost would be made public and serve as a measure of a bank's performance and accountability to its customers and the Central Economy Bank. It's important to note that a lower deficit or cost doesn't necessarily indicate a more efficient bank. These lending and borrowing rates would remain fixed, and the specific number could be arbitrarily determined. However, it's crucial to understand that the higher this arbitrary number, the greater its impact on the pricing of pre-identified products or services produced and consumed within the economy. All Bonafide deposits and outgoing interest payments at 11% per annum tax-free would be 100% guaranteed by the bank, with two conditions: that the money is transacted digitally, cannot be encashed in any currency, and not used for speculative purposes. In the PODS economy, where all banks are part of the government sector, managing money becomes a seamless process. Each bank essentially operates as a branch of the Central Economy Bank. When individuals or firms apply for loans or deposits, they are effectively making these requests to the Central Economy Bank through its various "branches."

For India and its citizens, the first step would be to accurately identify and provide bank accounts to every Indian. This can be facilitated through the existing Unique Identification Number (UID), which in this case would serve as a unique bank account identifier (Aadhar Card I.D.). In the PODS system, each economic unit, whether an individual, family, or firm, is encouraged to have just one bank account. This approach avoids double-counting for payments and receipts and simplifies financial transactions.

Unlike the current banking system where only a limited amount is guaranteed by the bank (e.g., 5 lakh rupees in India), in PODS banking, all deposits and interest payments are 100% guaranteed. Additionally, since PODS operates as a cashless banking system, there is no need for multiple accounts or ATM cards for cash withdrawals.

8. The Equity Markets According To Pods

OPTION 1

In the PODS system, equity markets operate with specific checks and balances to ensure fair and transparent trading. One approach is to implement bull and bear checks for shares. Here's how it works:

1. Initial Share Issuance: Let's take the example of a firm, M/S ABC, which issues its equity shares at INR 10 per share at time zero.
2. Year 1: In the first year, M/S ABC pays a dividend of INR 2 per share to its shareholders. At this point, a bear check is set at INR 12 per share, meaning that the share price cannot fall below this level.
3. Market Speculation: Investors and speculators can now make informed decisions based on the share's performance. They may speculate that M/S ABC's shares, given their history of INR 2 in dividends, could potentially rise to INR 14 per share in the future. This is an example of a bullish outlook.

4. Year 2: In the second year, M/S ABC decides to award a bonus share for each share held by investors, effectively increasing the bear check to INR 22 per share (10 + 2 + 10). Investors who had initially chosen INR 14 as their long call missed out on this opportunity. An interim dividend of INR 8 per share is also awarded, ensuring that profit and loss are balanced. The share price is directly influenced by the real earnings and commercial activity of M/S ABC.
5. Economic Sense: This approach ensures that equity shares are backed by actual physical production of goods, agricultural products, and services, rather than being purely speculative or driven by paper futures. Share pricing becomes a function of real earnings and economic activity.

By implementing bull and bear checks, PODS seeks to create a more stable and grounded equity market where prices are driven by genuine economic performance rather than speculative trading.

What if there is a loss? In the PODS stock market model, a loss in the value of shares is addressed in a way that ensures the real value of shares is maintained and that speculation is controlled. Here's how it works:

1. Addressing Losses: If a company, like M/S ABC, incurs a loss, say, INR 3 per share in the third year, the real value of each share becomes INR 19 (10 + 2 + 2 + 8 - 3) per share. At this point, the bear check prevents the share price from falling lower, but the bull check is still in effect.
2. Controlling Speculation: The system checks both bullish and bearish tendencies in the market. While

the bears cannot drive the share price lower than INR 19, the bulls are also constrained in their expectations. This balanced approach ensures that stock prices are grounded in actual commercial activity.

3. Dissolution of Failing Companies: If a company's equity shares end up at or below "0," they are required to be wound up and dissolved immediately. This ensures that companies with consistently poor performance do not linger in the market.
4. Additional Value: Any instruments issued by a company out of its profits or surpluses to create additional value can be added to its stock value. Cash surpluses can also be included, accounting for potential interim dividends or bonuses.

This stock market model aims to create a fair and stable system where the value of shares is based on real economic performance. It discourages excessive speculation and ensures that the total value of all shares listed on the stock market reflects the actual state of the economy.

Regarding mergers and acquisitions, under this model, traditional stock valuation systems may not apply in the same way. The focus is on real economic value, and mergers and acquisitions would need to align with this perspective. Example: If M/S ABC's manufacturing plant costs INR 1,20,00,000/- and assuming a 50: 50 split between debt & equity, there would be INR 6 million of debt & INR 6 million in equity (600,000 shares of INR 10/- per share at par value).

Using the previous various earnings as dividends & bonus issues and losses, the total value & investment in M/S ABC will be as follows:

In year one: debt INR 6 million (assuming no payback of debt principal). The equity value would be INR 7.2 million (INR 10 + 2 x 600,000 shares).

In year two: debt remains the same (assuming no payback of debt principal again), the equity value would be INR 13.2 million. Assuming the debt again to be static, the value of equity would fall to INR 11.4 million (13.2 million less 3 X 600000=1.8 million=11.4 million).

If someone were to merge or acquire M/S ABC, the true equity value would be INR 11.4 million for all 600,000 equity shares only. Interests on debt & depreciation have been factored into the P & L account and dividend & bonus pay-outs were made. A devaluation of the shares was also ordered when an INR 1.8 million loss was made in the third year. Note that because of PLIs there is no deduction of capital to be returned as M/S ABC met all quality, quantity & personnel targets. Its INR 3/- loss in the third year was excused because the war had broken out and a physical supply of semiconductors was not available. In the current system (minus all the jargon) if one started trying to acquire M/S ABC at a valuation which actually is far more than the cost of making a new plant similar to M/S ABC's existing plant capacity, it would be better to make a brand new plant because at the end of the day, there would be another physical new plant backing the money spent on it, vis a vis someone paying an exorbitant premium to take over the existing plant and creating nothing physically extra for this premium. Debt for just acquiring or merging an existing plant is worse than debt for an altogether new plant, as extra new capacity will back that debt. Not only that, but the new plant can also & will factor in the latest technological advancements & refinements in the new capacities that are created.

OPTION 2

In considering the financing structure for firms under the PODS model, the focus is on responsible and efficient capital allocation. This approach considers the cumulative earnings generated by a company throughout its existence. These earnings can be utilized in two primary ways: through equity or debt financing.

If a company opts for equity financing, it means issuing shares to raise capital. In this scenario, the company has multiple shareholders, and management is accountable to all these shareholders collectively. However, the PODS model introduces checks and balances to ensure equity prices are not manipulated. There are defined thresholds, both on the upside (Bull check) and downside (Bear check), which prevent shares from being traded beyond certain limits. This helps maintain realistic and stable valuations based on the company's actual performance.

Alternatively, the model allows for the conversion of cumulative earnings into debt. This debt is backed by the company's historical earnings and carries a fixed annual interest rate of 11%, paid out tax-free. Importantly, this debt cannot be used for speculative purposes and must be transacted digitally, guaranteeing 100% digital usage.

This raises an intriguing question: if a company like M/S ABC had chosen to rely solely on debt instead of issuing equity, would the cumulative payouts be more or less than servicing equity? In a debt-based scenario, management would primarily be answerable to debt holders, simplifying the accountability structure. On the other hand, equity financing entails being accountable to a broader base of shareholders.

Furthermore, the model scrutinizes the value proposition of mergers and acquisitions. It questions whether the enormous sums spent on acquisition deals, often advised by financial experts, are justified. For instance, two telecom giants, one in India and the other in Africa, were advised to merge at a staggering cost of USD 12 billion. This decision raised concerns as to whether the funds could have been more wisely invested in expanding capacity. Would this not be a burden on the value of the INR vis a vis the USD that would affect the valuations in the FX markets?

In the PODS model, the concept of debt is redefined to be at a zero-interest rate, as it operates within a no-profit, no-loss accounting framework. This approach effectively controls excessive greed and fraudulent practices. It emphasizes responsible financial management and value creation over profiteering. To illustrate, consider the scenario where an Indian company initially missed out on the opportunity to capture a significant market in India while contemplating the acquisition of an African firm for USD 24 billion. Subsequently, another Indian company invested USD 16 billion and acquired 408.7 million users in the Indian market. This example underscores the importance of strategic decisions and market insights in the business world. Even when individuals accumulate vast wealth, like Bill Gates, they often find that money alone cannot satisfy their deeper aspirations. Bill Gates, one of the world's wealthiest individuals, has redirected much of his wealth towards philanthropic causes, recognizing that excessive wealth can be emotionally taxing.

The overarching principle in the PODS model is that money is a powerful tool, but its value is ultimately determined by how it is used and what it contributes to society. It transcends the distinctions between various financial actors, whether they are involved in banking, stock trading, investment, entrepreneurship, or other economic activities. The key question is whether these activities result in the production or provision of pre-identified products or services that benefit society.

In the context of the PODS model, speculation is not the focus of economic activities, and instead, it encourages a more responsible and value-driven approach to finance. Speculative activities are not discouraged entirely, but they are channeled differently. For instance, in PODS-administered India, speculation takes place annually during Diwali, allowing individuals to engage in such activities during a designated time and within a controlled environment.

Furthermore, the equity market model described earlier in this framework minimizes the need for extensive regulations on compensation styles or systems. The inherent checks within the system are designed to prevent excessive compensation based on speculative volatility. This approach ensures that compensation is tied to real economic performance rather than speculative gains.

PODS offers a critical perspective on economics, particularly in contrast to traditional financial systems. For example, China's economic development, driven by government support for manufacturing and production, has led to a situation where it holds substantial Non-Performing Assets (NPAs) in its banking sector. Despite this, China's currency retains value due to the robust backing provided by its productive capacity.

It's worth noting that China only introduced its stock market in the early 2000s, after decades of emphasizing production-focused policies. China's massive reserves, if leveraged with international banks, could potentially influence global economies. However, the monopoly of currency issuance by countries like the USA means that settling these outstanding amounts would be relatively straightforward under the PODS banking system, as it involves just a few digital ledger entries.

Observations of central banks' actions reveal complex dynamics in the global financial landscape, where major currencies like the dollar, pound, and euro are strategically managed to maintain their value. These insights underscore the need for a more transparent and value-driven financial paradigm like PODS.

9. Pods And Barter - Beginnings

The economic evolution, starting from the barter system, can be envisioned in a futuristic PODS economy, leading to the emergence of unique monopolies—BENEPOLIES. These monopolies, adhering to the PODS model, predominantly involve goods, agros, and services, with also a focus on luxury offerings. Let's explore the BENEPOLIES across various sectors:

Food:

- Monopoly: M/s ODANA
- Signature Product: ODANA Brand Basmati Rice
- Associated Luxury: Clothes by M/s FASHWASH (crafted from original agro-based cloth materials)

Water:

- Monopoly: M/s H TWO OWE
- Signature Product: H-2-O Brand Mineral Water

Shelter:

- Monopoly: M/s CON-V-CON
- Signature Product: Prefab Houses

Education:

- Monopoly: M/s INTELLIGENCE
- Signature Product: Directly Brain Unloadable Education Subject-wise Systems (Pen drives)

Health:

- Monopoly: M/s AYURVEDA
- Signature Product: LALPLUS Health Package

Judiciary Services:

- Monopoly: M/s TARAZOO Services

Transport:

- Monopoly: M/s MERCEDES
- Signature Product: A to Z Model of Cars

In this barter economic scenario, each BENEPOLY invites applications for its products/services on a First Come First Served basis. Once all applications are supplied and accounted for by their respective banks, a lottery/auction is conducted for surplus products/services. The lottery represents the actual production and physical supply surplus, ensuring a fair distribution of these luxury offerings.

In practical examples of the BENEPOLIES' lottery system:

MERCEDES:

- Booked: 100 one-unit applications for Model V cars.
- Issued lottery numbers: 101 to 125 for the surplus production of 25 vehicles.

ODANA:

- Booked: 100 one-unit applications for 500 grams of ODANA brand rice per day for a year.
- Issued lottery numbers: 101 to 151 for the surplus production of 51 rice packs due to a bumper crop.

H TWO OWE:

- Booked: 100 one-unit applications for 2 litres of H-2-O brand mineral water per day for a year.
- Issued lottery numbers: 101 to 125 for the surplus production of 25 bottles due to excess rainfall.

CON-V-CON:

- Booked: 100 one-unit applications for pre-fab houses.
- Issued lottery numbers: 101 to 156 for the surplus production of 56 extra bedrooms cum bathroom units.

INTELLIGENCE:

- Booked: 100 one-unit applications in Graduate level courses in Planet Engineering.
- Issued lottery numbers: 101 to 200 for the surplus production of 100 extra direct unloadable courses in Gradual Planet Energy Planning.

AYURVEDA:

- Booked: 100 one-unit applications for LAL PLUS brand of Health Services.
- Issued lottery numbers: 101 to 134 for the surplus production of 34 "One-year hibernation" Pills.

TARAZOO Services:

- Booked: 100 one-unit applications for Calamity Insurance during hibernation.
- Issued lottery numbers: 101 to 111 for the surplus production of 11 service packs delivering claims to bank accounts.

In our ongoing economic scenario, we started with 100 economic units. As the economy progresses in real-time, producing and delivering products and services to the applied-for 100 economic units, the producers aim for maximum production with full capacity utilization, regardless of current sales. Surplus products are then taken up by banks and offered to the public through applications or lottery systems.

Now, here's a new development: 10 immigrants are permitted to enter the economy. Additionally, the export of some surplus is allowed, and in return, a new pre-identified product will be introduced into the economy (the specifics of which are currently a state secret). These immigrants are not just entering the economy; they are here to work as domestic help for the citizens of this PODS economy. The immigrants, being human, soon find themselves in need of the natural necessities (NN) mentioned earlier. Surpluses are then exchanged through a barter system using lottery numbers. For example, an immigrant might exchange a lottery ticket for a lottery number for a 2- liter pack of H-2-O brand mineral water (No. 111), a 500-gram pack of ODANA brand rice (No. 101), or even a V Model Mercedes (No. 113).

The logic behind these exchanges is that the supply of 2 liters of H-2-O water and 500 grams of ODANA rice per day will sustain the immigrant domestic help for a year until her visa comes up for renewal. Owning a Mercedes V Model, on the other hand, serves no immediate purpose until then. When the time comes for the immigrant to renew her visa, she might consider applying for her own Mercedes V model or possibly remitting it back to her original economy. Alternatively, she could persuade her employer to exchange another lottery number for any one of the surplus 7 products or services in return for a Mercedes V model.

It was leaked by the media that the new pre-identified product is a Domestic Robot. As a result, the immigrant domestic help is not granted a visa extension after one year. Instead, she contemplates various options, such as remitting a Mercedes V model as compensation for her one year of work in a PODS barter economy's citizen's prefab home, where she lived in an extra bedroom cum bathroom.

She begins to consider the possibility of hibernating for five years, convincing her employer to exchange M/s AYURVEDA's surplus One Year Hibernation Pills. To ensure her family's well- being in case she doesn't wake up after five years, she also contemplates convincing her employer to take M/s TARAZOO's Calamity Insurance during hibernation and provide her home economy's bank account details. In this scenario, she is allowed to hibernate for five years, and staying in this period is a prerequisite for authorities to consider citizenship.

Furthermore, she considers asking her employer, who feels indebted to her, to exchange his one original education capsule on Planet Engineering from M/s INTELLIGENCE, along with the Gradual Planet Energy Planning capsule. The idea is to use the Mercedes V model connected by a software matrix space highway to travel to another planet, rather than returning to her non-PODS economy. She even thinks about bringing some family members along for the journey.

The Mercedes V Model comes with an array of impressive features. Firstly, it operates on a Cold Nuclear Fusion Engine, allowing it to cover an extensive distance of 25 light years without the need for refueling. When cruising on inter-space highways, it offers three speed modes: a rapid acceleration to the speed of light in 2.5 seconds, a threefold increase to the speed of light in 6 seconds, and a maximum speed of 31 times the speed of light in just 1 minute. On planetary roads, it maintains a fixed speed of 55 mph for intercity travel and can accelerate to 1000 mph on interstate roads. The vehicle's versatility is remarkable, enabling it to fly, sail, and drive on regular roads while also smoothly navigating interspace warp highways. In terms of storage, its trunk can cleverly manage and store five distinct human environments, complete with provisions such as "water & rice" for a decade. The storage mechanism utilizes cutting-edge "shrink pack" technology, breaking down materials into memories stored in biochemical electronic packs. This process can be reversed, recreating physical items from their stored memories. This innovative approach draws parallels with how the human brain processes and retains information, ensuring efficient storage and retrieval of materials. In the context of PODS, a unique evolution can be witnessed, demonstrating an actual barter economic system. Benepolies, equipped with PLIs from banks due to surpassing their quality, quantity, and employment (QQE) targets, are incentivized to engage in production. Knowing that any excess production will be consumed and compensated for by banks, these entities are motivated to increase output, leading to additional income for both the businesses and their personnel.

This evolution extends to a comprehensive barter exchange system where valid allotment/applications become tradable commodities across goods, produce, services, and agros. This exchange is solely based on mutual needs and wants, emphasizing voluntary transactions. Like the replacement of currency denominations with application/allotment numbers, this barter trade is influenced by considerations of consumer surplus. In essence, it mirrors the fluidity of various currencies in exchange for goods or services, highlighting the adaptable nature of the economic framework.

10. Pods V/S Btt V/S Mmt

In comparing PODS with BTT (Banking Transaction Tax), it's crucial to understand their fundamental differences. BTT is a proposed taxation model where income tax is eliminated, and revenue for the government relies solely on the tax collected through banking transactions. In contrast, PODS issues digital money electronically, backed by future-produced assets such as healthy, satisfied, and employed citizens, goods, services and agros.

PODS operates without the constraints imposed by a taxation system like BTT. Digital money under PODS is not tied to gold or a currency basket; instead, its value is derived from tangible and essential elements, goods, services and agros produced in the economy. The production lag, theoretically assumed away, may be short enough in practice to avoid inflation.

Comparatively, PODS is lighter on the digital electronic infrastructure needed because transactions do not necessarily require recording due to the absence of taxation. Monitoring production- consumption matches becomes the primary focus, ensuring a continuous balance. BTT, on the other hand, operates as an automated system, potentially creating fewer jobs.

In the BTT system, the government is accountable to citizens for their spending since they are taxed. In PODS, where money is consistently available and the government doesn't impose taxes, accountability is arguably reduced except on the supply side—at least until elections, where the government's performance is judged based on the quality of past spending on the public and themselves rather than promises.

A noteworthy concern with BTT is that it might incentivize more cash transactions, contrary to the trend towards cashless transactions. In summary, while BTT relies on taxing transactions, PODS introduces a novel economic model without the burden of taxation, emphasizing balance and production-consumption matches.

Modern Monetary Theory (MMT) V/S PODS

Modern Monetary Theory (MMT) is a macroeconomic theory that views currency as a public monopoly and posits that unemployment indicates a restriction in the supply of financial assets by a currency monopolist. However, some critics argue that MMT is more of a fallacy, citing its unrealistic and non-traditional approach. However, PODS is more of an out of the box macroeconomic solution.

In contrast to the traditional economic approach, which involves creating a budget and adhering to it, MMT suggests a different path. It proposes the creation of money, for instance, to compensate for unemployment, setting rules that deem budget deficits acceptable and suggesting that national debt is not a cause for concern in any economy if the 'supply side' is maintained in balance with the 'demand side'.

While this approach may seem unconventional and somewhat delusional, it raises concerns about the potential for hyperinflation. The example of Zimbabwe in 2008, which experienced hyperinflation, serves as a cautionary tale against the unchecked implementation of such theories. Critics argue that the unrestricted creation of money and deficits might lead to economic instability and inflationary pressures, undermining the viability of MMT as a practical economic model, especially if supply side doesn't keep up with the objective of supporting the money printed.

In her book "The Deficit Myth," Professor Stephanie Kelton, former chief economist of the US Senate budget committee, provides insights into Modern Monetary Theory (MMT), characterizing it primarily as a description of the workings of modern fiat currency—the currency established by a government as legal tender for its citizens' transactions. This theory prompts a fundamental question: If the government possesses the authority to create money, what is the necessity for taxes? While acknowledging concerns about inflation, MMT suggests that the government can generate money for public initiatives and employment, provided there is unused economic capacity.

The conventional notion that government spending relies exclusively on citizen taxes is challenged by Kelton, who dismisses it as a "pure fantasy." Instead, MMT proposes a broader perspective, advocating for a nuanced understanding of the role of taxes in modern monetary policy. Taxes, according to MMT, have dual functions: they instill confidence in a government-backed currency, and they function to withdraw money from the economy.

Contrary to the idea that government spending should mirror tax collections, MMT opposes the balanced budget concept. It argues for a dynamic budgeting approach that adjusts to economic conditions, injecting or withdrawing money from the economy as needed to effectively manage inflation and unemployment. In essence, Professor Stephanie Kelton's perspective challenges traditional views on the relationship between taxes and government spending, offering a framework that emphasizes the government's capacity to create money and calls for a flexible budget aligned with economic realities.

Each of the economic models has its unique approach to managing currency and addressing economic challenges.

MMT challenges traditional notions by emphasizing the government's ability to create money, focusing on the real resources available in the economy rather than a gold standard. Critics express concerns about potential hyperinflation, a viewpoint that highlights the polarized opinions within mainstream economics.

On the other hand, PODS introduces an intriguing concept by eliminating traditional taxes and ensuring one hundred percent guarantee on deposits and interest payments, provided they are transacted digitally without speculation. This approach aims to prevent misuse and introduces a different paradigm in banking.

Comparing the two, PODS seems to prioritize digital transactions and guarantees, offering a unique solution to taxation concerns. Whether it's superior, especially in democracies, depends on the specific values and goals of a society. Democracies often value transparency, fairness, and citizen representation. PODS' emphasis on digital transactions and guarantees might align well with these principles. However, it's essential to consider the practical implementation, adaptability, and acceptance of such models in real-world economies. Experimenting with innovative economic theories can lead to valuable insights and improvements in existing systems. The key is finding a balance that ensures stability, fairness, and economic growth. Would you agree that PODS is superior, especially in democracies?

11. Mom-And-Pop Shops Versus Walmart Superstores

Picture the retail landscape as a duel between Mom-and-Pop shops and colossal Walmart-style superstores. The Mom & Pop shop, a cozy corner store, prioritizes a personalized, convenient shopping experience over cutthroat prices. On the flip side, the Walmart superstore lures customers with bulk discounts and an array of choices.

Now, imagine both sourcing their goods from the same local wholesale market. The Mom & Pop shop, ingenious in its approach, takes a 100 kg bag of rice, divides it into 100 one-kilogram bags, and competes pricewise with the supermarket. While the supermarket flexes its purchasing power, securing goods at wholesale rates, the Mom & Pop shop shows that, at times, local charm can rival the economic muscle of a retail giant. It's a retail tale where size doesn't always dictate success. What are your thoughts on the balance between small local businesses and retail giants?

In this analogy, the gross offerings of a Mom & Pop shop correspond to a single department in a supermarket, emphasizing that the number of items may be the same, but the scale differs. For instance, the Mom & Pop shop might boast 1000 diverse items overall, while the supermarket dedicates the same count solely to soap brands within its Special Soap Department. With 30 comparable Mom & Pop shops in the vicinity, one could explore the prospect of inviting them to collectively own equity in the larger supermarket and work as well along with their employees in a department of the superstore.

This collaborative ownership model envisions the Mom & Pop shops functioning as both employees and employers. A survey could ascertain whether this integration might result in increased, decreased, or stable incomes compared to their existing standalone operations. The analysis would then guide the decision on whether to maintain multiple Mom & Pop shops or consolidate into a centralized Supermarket. The recommendation is to involve all affected parties, primarily those in the Mom & Pop shops, in the decision-making process, ensuring their perspectives shape the outcome.

In an alternative scenario, regardless of whether the shops are Mom & Pop establishments or Super Shops, a system of "equalization" is proposed. Under this model, the public pays a fixed income to the shopkeeper(s), which represents a markup on the costs incurred by the shopkeeper for procuring goods and services (at actuals), in addition to the amount charged to the customer. Shoddy service or inadequate availability of products and services, unless attributed to issues at the producer or manufacturer level, would result in penalties for the shopkeeper(s). It's worth noting that a vigilant network of Demand Monitors, Supply Monitors, and Economic Coordinators constantly oversees all the products and services offered in these shops.

12. Economic/Industrial Life-Cycles

In examining various product/service life cycles, including their Industry Life Cycles (ILC), a common pattern emerges, consisting of introductory, growth, maturity, and decline stages. Let's delve into these stages and consider renaming the last stage, assuming PODS is the chosen economic mode.

Before the Introductory Stage, there is a discovery phase for a pre-identified product or service with commercial potential. This discovery prompts the administrators of an economy to take it up for supply to economic units. Subsequently, the mass production engineering stage unfolds, with Demand Monitors taking charge of assessing and reporting the required quantities from the Supply Monitors. The primary objective here is achieving Manufacturing Capacity Growth up to Full Supply. Different suppliers of the same product or service compete to reach Full Supply, thereby achieving maturity as reliable providers across various price bands and quality benchmarks.

The traditional Decline stage of a pre-identified product or service is replaced in the PODS context. Instead, it transitions into the Supply of The New Model of that product/service. Beyond that, there is the Replacement market for the updated product/service, exploring New Uses, and Realignment of the product/service to current market conditions and environments. Planning for such dynamic industrial life cycles, like the evolution from film to digital cameras or the emergence of selfies from cell phones, poses a challenge but underscores the adaptability required in this economic model.

The emergence of the Latest Product or Service Model Economy (LMEs) becomes evident through historical trends. However, I hold the view that supplying LMEs might not align with good manufacturing practices or natural consumption, as it often leads to induced consumption. Take the example of Cars – how many different models or varieties can one have? The automotive industry already boasts an overwhelming array of models and types. In today's market, there are entire TV programs dedicated to helping consumers navigate the plethora of choices. While variation and improvement are essential aspects of product development, these features and experiences could be consolidated in real-time milestones, pre-determined among various product or service criteria. This approach avoids the need for a new model for every "annual automobile show" and promotes more sustainable and consumer-friendly practices.

Consider the evolution of transportation needs, for instance:

1. Requirement/Discovery: The need for speedy transport of humans from Place A to Place B is identified and included in the basket of pre-identified products/services for manufacturing and supply.

2. Product and Service Introduction: The Ford Model T car is introduced, and assembly line factories are established for production engineering.
3. Market Saturation and Issues: After producing millions of cars, motor vehicular emissions are acknowledged as a negative environmental impact. Despite this, many car models continue to be manufactured, leading to environmental concerns.
4. Technological Advances: Changes in engine technology enable the production of new "Clean Cars" to address environmental issues.
5. Ongoing Challenges: The market never achieves saturation, and emissions from cars persist. "Smaller cars" have been introduced, resembling two-wheelers, to cater to the masses.
6. Current Need: There is a growing demand for more "Clean Cars" due to increased environmental awareness.
7. Obstacles in Meeting Current Need: The missing element is the first "P" - proactive action. Alternatively, funding can be sought from the Indian Global Changeover Bank (IGCB). With PODS in place, Clean Cars would have been readily available once the pollution issue was recognized, emphasizing the importance of proactive measures in addressing environmental concerns.

When considering the transition to cleaner technologies, it's crucial to address the impact on industries heavily invested in fossil fuel-powered technologies. Specifically, manufacturers of fossil-fueled combustion engines may need to undergo significant changes or realign their focus toward producing "Clean Engines/Motors." Similarly, fossil hydrocarbon liquid fuel manufacturers may face displacement, but alternative and beneficial uses for these fuels, particularly crude petroleum oil, should be explored.

To encourage a smooth transition and avoid economic disruptions, efforts can be directed towards motivating these vested interests to adapt. For instance:

Funding for Engine Manufacturers: Companies specializing in combustion engines could receive financial support to shift their production to electric motors for electric-powered cars. Their existing combustion engines could be repurposed as backup engines or for start-up purposes in Clean Cars.

Diversification of Fossil Hydrocarbon Liquid Fuel Makers: Manufacturers of fossil hydrocarbon liquid fuels could consider diversifying their operations. Instead of focusing solely on fuel production, they could repurpose their capacities to produce crude petroleum-based PVC/plastic/polymer pipes. These pipes could then be utilized in the development of global and country-specific water delivery and management systems designed for precise human, agricultural, industrial, and treatment applications.

This approach aims to balance the need for environmental sustainability with the economic considerations of existing industries, fostering a transition that is both environmentally conscious and economically viable.

To facilitate the transition to cleaner technologies and support industries in their conversion efforts, the Indian Global Changeover Bank (IGCB) can play a crucial role. However, there are certain conditions to be considered, such as the valuation of a barrel of oil. If the valuation exceeds the average value of oil since its discovery, and inflation is not factored in, the cost of conversions, whether in the production of crude petroleum-based PVC/plastic/polymer pipes or the manufacturing of electric motors, would be covered by the IGCB.

Additionally, there is a call for prioritizing and funding research and development (R&D) in Nuclear Cold Fusion and engines powered by this fusion as the next level of energy. This signifies a shift toward sustainable and advanced energy sources.

With the incorporation of the first "P" (Pre-identified Products/Services) and the proposed Product/Industry Life Cycles (PLC/ILC), products and services are expected to evolve, consolidating into brands of the highest quality. The determination of quality criteria and parameters will be a collaborative effort between producers and consumers, shaped by real-time experiences in production and consumption.

Concerning pricing, the cost for the best quality brand will be calculated based on total expenses incurred or required for manufacturing only the best brand, divided by the number of units to be produced and sold. This calculated figure will serve as the asking price for the best quality brand. With PODS in effect, there will be sufficient monetary provisions in both the demand and supply pipelines for pre-identified products and services. Using the example of cars:

1. Demand Pipeline: Adequate monetary provisions will be available to support the demand for high-quality cars.
2. Supply Pipeline: Manufacturers will have the necessary funds to produce these high-quality cars, meeting the demand and maintaining a balanced economic ecosystem.

While the theoretical framework of No Loss No Profit-Best Quality-Affordable Price for a pre- identified product and service, such as a car, seems promising, practical challenges and considerations arise. It raises questions about whether everyone is entitled to purchase a 100% Zero Emissions Mercedes with a backup and start-up petrol/diesel engine at an affordable price. Achieving a full supply saturation market state globally for any pre-identified product or service, as exemplified by Germany to some extent, remains a challenge.

The concept of "PURR," denoting Product Usage Responsibility Regulations, introduces the idea that manufacturers, especially of potentially dangerous goods and services, should be held accountable for the use of their products. For instance, if there were no RDX or similar products, the existence of suicide bombers might be mitigated. "PURR" suggests that manufacturers of such products should bear responsibility for their misuse.

Applying this principle to Mercedes, the question arises: Should Mercedes be allowed to form itself into a BENEPOLY, essentially an Allowed Monopoly for the manufacture of cars in India's PODS mode? This could position Mercedes as a Global Market Pre-Identified Product and Service Preferred Supplier/Manufacturer under the PODS system. This strategic alignment could contribute to customers benefiting from the ability to purchase a car that offers optimal sustained satisfaction as both a product and a service, all at an affordable price.

13. Few Words On Competition

Competition is often misunderstood and misused, creating negativity around the concept. In my perspective, competition only truly exists when a market reaches saturation or Full Supply. For instance, when everyone already owns a TV, attempting to sell or market another TV becomes a competitive scenario. Until this point of market saturation is reached, the focus should shift towards consumers who do not yet own TVs. Subsequently, the introduction of a New Model or catering to the Replacement Market becomes the next phase in the competitive landscape.

This brings us to a crucial question: understanding the dynamics of demand and production in any market, past, present, or future, with the goal of achieving Full or Total Supply. Particularly for products and services addressing "natural needs" (NN), the key challenge is identifying the point at which desires become so compelling that individuals go to great lengths to satisfy them, even when their needs are already met.

The argument advocating that only prices for "natural needs" (NN) goods, products, or services should contribute to an Inflation or Deflation Index is rooted in the belief that NN items represent essential requirements, while the rest fall into the categories of wants, desires, or luxuries beyond a certain price point. The ultimate economic goal here is to achieve and sustain zero inflation or a deflationary scenario specifically for NN goods. This aligns with the envisioned state of a PODS system, emphasizing real-time objectives and targets for NN categories, with the aim of continuing this state indefinitely.

14. Note On Logistics

The acceptability of a deflation number below zero is contingent on its impact on lowering prices in the "natural needs" (NN) group of goods and services. However, it's crucial that income levels remain unaffected or, ideally, increase despite this deflation number. This scenario can be achieved if non-wage or non-salary/income components contributing to the costs of NN products decrease due to efficiencies in economies of scale. The resultant cost savings can then be passed on to deflate the price of NN items, leading to a rise in real income for wages, salaries, or incomes. It's recommended that the Inflation & Deflation index be area-specific, taking into account location, and incorporating logistical and packaging considerations for NN pricing.

For instance, if the cost of transporting Rice from Punjab to Rajasthan involves lorry freight, a subsidy or equalization should be applied uniformly across various logistical distances or other cross sections of logistical costs. This could entail adding, for example, INR 1100/- per metric ton to the actual consumer price for a metric ton of Rice throughout the economy, regardless of the real cost and the logistical distances or other factors between the producer of Rice and its ultimate consumer. The logistic cost should be an averaged-out figure, with compensation provided to those incurring additional burdens on logistical costs and refunds to those experiencing lower costs in the same logistical aspects. Achieving a balance in this account is a complex task, and the surplus or deficit on account of the "Cost of/in Logistics" would be determined by the intricacies of the logistics involved.

The discussion on the Costs of Logistics and how to handle them will evolve and be determined in real-time, particularly when PODS achieves saturation in natural need (NN) goods. Ultimately, each factory producing a lorry will have a similar cost ex-plant, and the competitiveness of the plant will hinge on its proximity to specific markets. In the long run, logistics, concerning the transportation of NNs from production to consumption areas/points, will become a crucial pricing and costing determinant. The packaging aspect will also be a noteworthy cost to consider. The 7 + 2 "P"s have already addressed these issues to some extent.

15. How Many Choices?

The number of choices available per product or service can indeed influence the type of market economy. Let's take the example of apples: if you consume two apples a day and suddenly get them for free, the consumption might vary. Some might stick to two, some might consume more, and others might consume less.

Now, consider the variety of apples in the market. In a scenario with numerous types or brands of apples, we could refer to it as a Free Market Economy (FME). In contrast, if there are only, let's say, 10 different types or brands available (a Ten Market Economy=TME), the consumer has a more limited set of choices. The number of choices per product or service could determine the nature of the market economy. If there are 10 options, it's a TME, and one could potentially move to an Eleven Market Economy (EME) or down to an Eight Market Economy (ETME), depending on the variety offered. The flexibility to move between these economies reflects the dynamics of consumer choices and market conditions.

The number of choices available in a market, whether it's an Eleven Market Economy (EME), a Ten Market Economy (TME), or an Eight Market Economy (ETME), can influence individual consumption patterns. In an EME, one might have 11 brands/types of apples to choose from, while in an ETME, the choices might be limited to 8. The transition between these economies reflects the dynamism of consumer preferences and market conditions.

The balance between the quantity and quality of choices is a crucial aspect. More choices may lead to a potential pitfall where the quality between products and services becomes suspect. On the other hand, a limited number of high-quality choices can provide a different kind of satisfaction. The criteria for determining the optimal number for an economy are complex, often influenced by the population of economic units within that economy. A lower-populated economy may have the advantage of making better choices in terms of both quantity and quality.

The concept of branding is interesting. While corporates play a significant role in producing goods and services, economies provide the resources for production. It would be apt for products like apples to be branded based on their origin, such as "Made/Grown in India," as economies contribute to the conditions and resources for production. The intersection of corporate branding and national or regional origin adds layers to the identity of products and services.

It's evident to me that, regardless of the chosen number for the economy, let's say it declares itself an Eleven Market Economy (EME), there is a crucial need to invest resources in establishing a state of PODS. In this state, there must be an absolute and sustained equilibrium in meeting the Natural Needs (NN) for all economic units within the EME. This implies that all 11 varieties of NN, the "Natural Needs," should be consistently and adequately available to meet the needs of every economic unit. Adequacy here refers to both quantity and quality. Beyond achieving and sustaining this saturation in NN, I am open to considering any level of luxuries or desires. And I won't be alone in this sentiment until this sustained NN saturation is accomplished.

16. Differences Between The Rich And Poor

Let me share my observations on what I call "The Product Brand Caste System," which also serves to illustrate the distinction between The Rich and The Poor. Take, for instance: the Natural Needs (NN)-based Product/Brand-based caste system:

RICH/ POOR

1) Food

- Rice eats every day 4 times, only branded Basmati Rice
- gets to eat once a day shoddy Infested PDS rice

2) Clothes

- Numerous designer clothes
- One khadi kurta pajama, similar to hand made cotton shirt & pant

3) Water

- drinks only branded mineral water
- drinks water whose quality is suspect

4) Shelter

- Lives in a palatial house
- Lives in a Jhuggi Or, Village hut.

5)Education

- Goes to Delhi University India for Studies after Expensive boarding school
- Attends the village school whenever, A Teacher is available to teach and makes it to Delhi University India only on a Scholarship which he gets, thanks to PODS

6) Health

- John Hopkins University Hospital for Any & all treatment
- The Village quack or treatment at the local ESI infirmary/ Mohalla clinics/ government hospitals

7) Judiciary

- Access to the best lawyers in case of having to face any injustice
- hardly any access to any lawyer in case of any wrongdoing or injustice by others

8) Transport

- Travel in a chauffeur-driven Mahindra E-Car.

- Travel by Bus by buying a bus ticket. Or uses his own bicycle.

The distinction between the Rich and the Poor essentially boils down to a matter of comfort, where the Rich can indulge in premium brands of products and services, while the Poor are limited to more affordable and generic options.

17. The Hr Project

In a comprehensive Human Resources initiative, a ranking system will be implemented, assigning an Economic Level Rank to individuals, including Doctors, Lawyers, and all Indian citizens. This dynamic ranking will provide citizens with a clear indication of their standing in the economy, subject to fluctuations based on various criteria and parameters. Individuals sharing the same rank could exist, and this system could extend to large corporations and banks, allowing employees and employers to gauge an individual's position within the organization. Prospective customers, too, would be informed about the rank of the person they are interacting with, providing transparency and clarity. For Example, In this ranking system, individuals, including high-ranking officials like the President of a bank, would be assigned a rank based on their standing within the organization. For instance, the President of a bank with 100 employees might have a rank of 1/100. This system would extend to both a national economic rank level and a corporate (or relevant entity) employee rank level. The purpose of this ranking is to provide individuals with a clear understanding of their position compared to others and encourage the government or employer to take actions that would elevate an individual's rank if there was potential. The goal is to maximize the number of economic units achieving higher rank levels, although it's acknowledged that not everyone can be at the same rank level. Living at the same level as the least-paid employee, even for a day, is a mark of a true and worthy employer. It's worth noting that employees often extend credit to their employers until payday. In the world envisioned by Ayn Rand, there were efforts to establish corporations where employees also held ownership. Today, the landscape has evolved, with employees commonly receiving stock equity in the companies where they work as part of standard compensation packages. This coexistence of employees and employers, motivated and sustained, reflects a realization of Ms. Rand's vision. Rest in peace.

18. Army-War As An Example

The Armed or Defense Forces in India offer a compelling example of PODS. While they consume a significant portion of GDP, they don't produce tangible goods. The classic economic concept of "Guns & Butter" takes an interesting turn, with a potential shift to prioritizing "Bread & Butter," emphasizing basic needs over military expenditures.

The Microeconomics of PODS are available with modern defense forces. In India, for instance, under the pre-identified necessity product category "alcohol" in the economic basket of all armed personnel, they have got it down to "two" pegs of Rum per day in Winter, and "one" peg of Rum per day in Summer. "Old Monk" Rum only; just kidding...there are quite a few choices of Rum.

After enduring two world wars and numerous conflicts, it seems high time for the global community, especially the Dollar-centric world, to recognize that war ultimately benefits only those who initiate and orchestrate it. Soldiers return from the battlegrounds, having "won" the war, only to grapple with the profound impacts on their lives. It's crucial for nations to redirect their military capabilities toward protecting borders, homeland security, civil stability, and managing immigration. Exporting war is a perilous endeavor, as it can eventually circle back to one's own doorstep. Some regions persist in perpetuating this cycle, but the solution lies in acknowledging past wrongs, preventing their recurrence, and not succumbing to the destructive cycle of war. Those who profit from selling weapons to conflicting parties bear a heavy responsibility for the resulting carnage, surpassing even the buyers and users of those weapons in culpability. Enforcing comprehensive sanctions that restrict the supply of guns and bullets to rogue states could be a potent strategy to curb conflicts and promote peace. If such measures were rigorously applied to countries like Pakistan, Afghanistan, and Iraq, it could potentially hasten the resolution of ongoing conflicts. The scenario envisions a situation where a rogue state, deprived of a fresh supply of arms and ammunition, would exhaust its existing stocks. In the case of nuclear-armed nations like Pakistan, the focus shifts to preventing the use of these weapons. The suggestion is that even with nuclear capabilities, there is a belief that these arms wouldn't be directed at neighboring countries like India. Instead, in a war scenario, the deployment of nuclear arms might target coalition bases in the immediate vicinity, or potentially affect sovereign territories of coalition member states. The underlying premise is that the root cause of the conflicts lies in the abundance of weapons supplied by external entities, and cutting off this supply could bring about a more peaceful resolution.

The acquisition of weapons from external sources, often labeled as "Infidels," raises questions about the motives behind such purchases. The narrative questions who the greater INFIDEL is and suggests a broader perspective beyond religious conflicts. The key argument is that by refusing to buy "Guns & Bullets" from external suppliers, particularly those identified as INFIDELs, nations could potentially disrupt a lucrative economic activity centered around the arms trade. The message implies that the religion of war, representing the global phenomenon of conflict-driven economic, political, and business activities, needs to be comprehensively controlled to eliminate perpetual violence. Criticism is directed at the media, portrayed as more interested in reporting on war zones for increased viewership and revenue rather than actively contributing to peace efforts. The preference is expressed for media coverage of meetings aimed at halting wars, emphasizing the potential impact of such gatherings in promoting global harmony. Picture an unedited, live broadcast of a colossal meeting, spanning the entire duration it takes to address global issues— perhaps even surpassing the coverage duration of the tragic Mumbai 26/11 attacks. In this setting, all pertinent stakeholders, irrespective of their number, convene to engage in open discussions, utilizing words and speeches to thrash out and resolve issues. This unfiltered dialogue, involving 150,000-plus individuals, would be transmitted live across the entire planet, offering an alternative to scattered meetings fueled by "Guns & Bullets" and often resulting in no resolution other than the sacrifice, martyrdom, or duty, marked by the somber label: "Killed in Action."

Imagine a world where economic activity, not weapons, is the tool for enforcing lasting peace. In this vision, India takes a bold step by proposing a bill in the United Nations, advocating for a global ban on the sale and purchase of weapons among member countries or economies. The current scenario, where India, one of the largest arms importers, has started exporting weapons, raises concerns. The UN Security Council, responsible for diffusing security threats, should play a pivotal role in ensuring a world without the proliferation of arms.

Contrary to the trend of seeking a permanent seat on the UN Security Council, the proposal argues against India being a member. India's historical stance of refraining from aggressive overseas military actions aligns with the desire to maintain this principled position. The core belief is that restricting the availability of arms and munitions can prevent numerous conflicts and acts of terrorism.

As a global economist, the proposal suggests a novel approach: paying off arms and munitions manufacturers not to produce weaponry. The argument rests on the idea that the cost of human lives, trauma, and infrastructure destruction far exceeds the profits garnered by arms manufacturers. However, this approach allows manufacturers to produce arms exclusively for the UN Security Council members, ensuring a responsible and controlled deployment of military capabilities globally.

In this envisioned world, each UN Security Council member would be responsible for protecting neighboring countries against potential threats. For instance, China would safeguard India against Pakistan, and vice versa. Simultaneously, Security Council members are expected to refrain from supporting divisive forces or terrorists within other member countries.

For non-Security Council members, the focus of their defense forces would be confined to border and homeland security, with the explicit and implicit assurance of security cover from the UN Security Council's defense forces. This framework aims to establish a world where economic cooperation and diplomacy take precedence over the destructive consequences of armed conflicts.

The proposal takes a decisive stance on arms and munitions production by advocating for governments to pay off manufacturers not to engage in weapon production. This approach prioritizes the prevention of armed conflicts, emphasizing the economic efficiency of avoiding the costly aftermath of wars and civil strife.

The vision extends to resolving security issues through the intervention of UN Security Council forces, promoting a global reliance on diplomatic and cooperative measures rather than resorting to armed conflicts. The concept of Product Usage Responsibility Regulation (PURR) is proposed as a crucial framework to hold weapons manufacturers accountable for the consequences of their products.

Under PURR, manufacturers of destructive weapons, such as RDX, would be held responsible for any harm caused using their products, especially in acts of terrorism. The regulation seeks to enforce strict accountability on weapon manufacturers, ensuring punitive measures for any misuse or harm caused by their products. This approach aligns with the broader goal of fostering a world where responsible and ethical practices govern the production and use of weapons, with a strong emphasis on global peace and security.

19. Peace & Not Piece, Please

RUSSIA, USA, CHINA & INDIA should take the initiative to become friends with each other and make sure there is no war anywhere by not allowing weapons, arms & munitions to be sold except to the UN peacekeeping force, as well as to a joint outer space peace & defence keeping forces. Soldiers should be encouraged to psychologically remain secure without arms or other weapons. No "Guns & Butter".

In a PODS economy, the proposal underscores the importance of domestic defense forces maintaining neutrality with the government while being subservient and emphasizes the self- sufficiency of these forces in producing their own weapons. Politicians are urged to govern based on economic considerations rather than egos, refraining from aggressive posturing or emotional manipulation of defense forces to procure foreign weapons.

The proposal advocates for a shift in political leaders' mindsets, emphasizing the need to control egos and views. It introduces the idea that a lack of ego between individuals fosters love, and this love translates into politicians serving and provisioning the individuals they lead. This shift is facilitated by the absence of taxes in a PODS economy, where politicians and their administrations are not immediately answerable to the public for spending decisions. Accountability is deferred until the next elections, where leaders will be judged and re-elected based on their spending choices.

The political landscape in a PODS economy transcends traditional ideological divisions, with no communists, socialists, capitalists, or monarchies. Instead, all states operate as controlled democracies, with varying degrees of control. The proposal asserts that external forces should not interfere in the internal matters of any state, emphasizing the importance of maintaining sovereignty. Global human rights initiatives and institutions are established to monitor and address governance issues, ensuring checks and balances for leaders who may overstep their bounds.

PODS underscores its commitment to providing ample monetary resources without constraints, aligning with the availability of factual and real resources. This flexibility ensures that economies can meet their domestic needs at a high global standard. While imported goods are allowed, if necessary, trade and manufacturing transactions between two countries involve the use of each other's domestic currencies. The importing country pays in its currency, and the exporting country receives payment in its own currency through a neutral global intermediary. This system avoids a basket of currencies and instead utilizes all currencies.

In accordance with the PODS banking paradigm, held currencies accrue tax-free 10% interest per annum in domestic digital monies. These funds are not permitted for speculative purposes, and the full deposit along with interest is 100% guaranteed if the money is utilized digitally and for non- speculative activities. Importantly, the inflation or deflation rate is set at zero. Political propaganda should be restricted to domestic elections only and the era of political violence needs to come to an end. Peaceful and constructive political discourse is key to fostering a healthy democracy and ensuring the well-being of the citizens.

20. The Domestic And Foreign Exchange Rate Connection

Let's dive into the tangled world of currency valuations—a realm where traditional economic practices might need a serious reality check. The valuation of currencies against each other has been a contentious issue, with the traditional economic system allowing and manipulating what seems like a significant scam. Notably, the USA and the UK are running multi-trillion dollar/pound deficits, while China and Japan boast multi-trillion-dollar surpluses. Despite this, the US Dollar is valued against the Chinese Yuan at 7.14 per US Dollar, and the Japanese Yen at 143 per US dollar. The days of the US dollar and the British Pound hiding behind each other and dictating financial norms to the world are fading, though it's essential to acknowledge that they are not inherently malevolent.

21. A Few Aspects Of Pods

PODS offers a platform for genuine independent politicians, potentially operating without party affiliations and free from political biases. The economic landscape dictates politics universally, and with politicians having control over the Economy Mint and Currency, the need to raise funds from the public diminishes. Instead, they can request funds from the finance minister/department for spending in their constituencies on pre-identified products/services, aligning with the demand/supply and coordinated framework. All expenses, including personal ones, would be transparently recorded and scrutinized in local newspapers or magazines, fostering a system of good politics. Establishing good political leadership armed with PODS is crucial in the current global scenario. These leaders can assemble a team of MBAs and engineers in their constituencies to manufacture various pre-identified products and services. The process would be overseen by Demand & Supply Monitors and Economic Coordinators, forming the new PODS bureaucracy, ensuring strict compliance with PODS objectives. The cost of these monitors and coordinators can be justified by their adequate compensation, contingent on delivering PODS objectives without corruption or inefficiency. Failure to meet expectations will result in severe consequences. The ongoing hundred smart cities project in India exemplifies the practical implementation of this aspect of PODS.

Shifting to the PODS system raises questions about the capabilities of our MPs, as the previous constituency allowances often went unutilized. In transitioning to PODS, the immediate concern is determining the individuals responsible for allocating funds and overseeing the manufacturing of various products, such as Electrical Mercedes cars and H-2-O Mineral Water. This process must be equitable, fair, and transparent to ensure that those selected for these tasks contribute to job creation and economic activity. The introduction of "E" models exclusively for employees, even if they are defective cars repaired after rigorous inspection, adds another layer to India's PODS economy, alongside brands like Maruti Suzuki and the introduction of foreign technologies, exemplified by Tesla's influence in car technologies.

22. Tesla Or Mercedes First

To support this venture, Mercedes will have access to a substantial line of credit covering capital, funds, and land. Additionally, they are granted the freedom to hire as many MBAs and Engineers from India as they require, with visas facilitated for any personnel Mercedes wishes to send from abroad. The responsibility of executing the entire project in India has been delegated to a team of seven German citizens known as HQ 7. These individuals are dual trained in both engineering and business administration, having received education and instruction at the Mercedes School of Automobile Engineering, Management & Marketing (MSAEMM). They bring valuable experience from their work in engineering Mercedes cars.

The Ministry of Demand Monitors is now in the process of evaluating and determining the supply requirements for the upcoming commissioning of the new Mercedes plant on a 1000-acre plot in Greater Noida, near Delhi, India. Simultaneously, the Ministry of Supply Monitors initiates the opening of a line of credit at the nearby dedicated State Bank of India (IS= Invitation Services) Branch, designating all HQ 7 members as signatories.

HQ 7 is tasked with listing their local Indian personnel needs, and the Supply Monitors begin drafting the list of personnel requirements. HQ 7 indicates a need for 108 automobile engineers with MBA majors in production engineering and management. The Maruti Suzuki Institute of Automobile Engineering & Management (MSIAEM) is identified as a potential source with 200 students graduating in time for these vacancies.

Mercedes suggests relocating one of its German plants to Greater Noida, but the Supply Monitor expresses a preference for a new state-of-the-art plant, despite its complete automation. After deliberation, HQ and HQ 7 agree to this request, and to enhance the deal, the Supply Monitor increases the land parcel size to 2000 acres. This land is exclusively designated as The Invited German Mercedes Self-Contained Smart City Economic Zone. This zone is specifically and solely reserved for Mercedes from Germany. As a result, HQ 7 decides to accept the request for the latest state-of-the-art plant, and 12 additional German visas are requested for extra personnel.

It transpires that German banks & investors were not willing to fund this changeover into a new plant that would make state-of-the-art Zero Emission Cold Nuclear Fusion Engines.

Maruti Suzuki hears of this and applies to their Supply Monitor to request that the new Mercedes plant be approached to make state-of-the-art Cold Nuclear Fusion Engines for their Maruti Suzuki model cars.

At this time, German banks and Investors realized that Mercedes is opening a new engine plant in some place called Greater Noida in India; the same plant that was rejected by them to be made in place of the old plant which would be scavenged & scrapped. HQ & HQ 7 + 12 (HQ 19) rejoice in the news that they are being financed for a new plant in Germany and decided to go ahead and attempt & make 2 New Engine Plants. One in Germany & One in India. They also accepted the request from the Maruti Suzuki Supply Monitor (s), to make cold nuclear fusion engines for their Maruti Suzuki model cars.

It appears that German banks and investors initially hesitated to fund the transition to a new plant for state-of-the-art Zero Emission Cold Nuclear Fusion Engines. However, Maruti Suzuki, upon learning of this situation, approaches their Supply Monitor to suggest that the new Mercedes plant be considered for manufacturing state-of-the-art Cold Nuclear Fusion Engines for their Maruti Suzuki model cars.

Simultaneously, German banks and investors recognize that Mercedes is establishing a new engine plant in Greater Noida, India, the same plant they had rejected as a replacement for the old plant slated for scrapping. HQ, HQ 7, and the additional 12 personnel (HQ 19) celebrate the news of securing financing for a new plant in Germany. They decide to proceed with the ambitious plan of establishing two new engine plants—one in Germany and one in India. Furthermore, they accept the request from the Maruti Suzuki Supply Monitors to produce cold nuclear fusion engines for their cars.

A joint Research and Development (R&D) mission is initiated between the Mercedes School of Automobile Engineering, Management & Marketing (MSAEMM) and the Maruti Suzuki Institute of Automobile Engineering & Management (MSIAEM) to create a smaller two-wheeler "car" powered by a cold nuclear fusion engine for the Indian market.

HQ 7 selects 70 Engineer MBAs from MSIAEM, 26 Engineer MBAs transition from Maruti Suzuki, replaced by new hires from MSIAEM, and an additional 90 engineers are recruited to expand production. Fourteen individuals are chosen for the joint R&D mission. All Indian engineers undergo training under HQ 19 and participate in a Learning & Teaching Tour (LTT) at the German plant. Capital and funds are allocated to Maruti Suzuki to enhance production capacities, hire new graduates, and support the 14 individuals involved in the R&D mission. The R&D funds are overseen by the Economic Coordinators of both the Mercedes and Maruti Suzuki projects.

In this case, the new Mercedes plant in India is allowed to contribute from its No Loss No Profit P & L Account to the cost of the new Mercedes plant in Germany (in case required), that too, in Euros.

As this new plant was on the drawing table for the last 5 years, the entire plant details are available in enormous, detailed manuals, which record & list every minute sequential step in the production engineering, right from start of project to commissioning of project. The entire plant will be totally automated by robots. All components would be automatically assembled by robots. Some components would be sourced from Maruti Suzuki, while other component manufacturers would be invited by Mercedes itself to manufacture the same within its specific economic zone in Greater Noida, India.

Equitable, fair, and transparent enough! What say? Or, too ideal?

Now, to the domestic corporate M/s H TWO OWE (MHTO) the manufacturer of the H-2-O brand of mineral water:

MHTO is assigned a Demand monitor (DM) & a Supply monitor (SM) and Economic Coordinator (EC) between them. It is announced that all or any tenders that may be floated to upgrade MHTO's

Plant & Machinery and/or others, will be awarded only to the best tenderers only. Meaning, L1(lowest quotation) & T1(latest technology) will forever give way to B1(best quotation) & T1.

The DM & SM, assisted by the EC, review the existing plant & machinery and its capacity. After Demand is assessed & the required quality parameters are reported to the SM, the SM provides all the monies & resources that are required to build up to the reported quality & quantity numbers in actual production. The EC sees to it that the DM & SM work in perfect harmony and that the numerical objectives of quality & quantity are met within pre-stated time frames as provided in the CPM & decision tree analysis reports. However, due to power shortages, the management of MHTO reports to the SM that there are manufacturing constraints, and the numbers may not be met, The SM immediately sends in Generators to bridge the power shortage gap. Management immediately state that due to the added cost of the Generating sets (Gensets), the price of the H-2- O brand 2-liter bottle must be increased and insisted that the SM along with the DM & EC approach the power company to cater to provide the shortfall in power that MHTO's manufacturing plant is facing. The Power company is either asked to absorb the extra cost of generating power by MHTO or supply the same in due course by providing the Genset in the first place and bill power at the normal power rate to MHTO.

MHTO pays for power to the utility company based on a complex equation of quality, quantity, & productivity between labour/machinery & power, & consumer satisfaction indices; the higher (meaning positive) it is awarded, the lower (in terms of the power billing amounts) the utility expenses are accounted for in the MHTO accounts. All manufacturing units are billed for Power by this complex equation. In a similar manner, agriculture is also billed and the emphasis on lower power bills is directly related to the efficiency & productivity of the usage of supplied power. All these business environment permutations and combinations would have been provisioned for in the project CPM or Decision Tree Analysis.

Basic power needs are assessed by a DM, and the SM & EC are made to supply these at Zero billing amounts; voluntary usage over these minimum power allowances is and will be billed at Cost (this is because we are in a No-profit-No-loss accounting system). The Power Company which has the lowest Cost; of their personnel is given bonuses when compared to each other (The costs of different Power companies with each other) based on the actual accounted differences in costs.

All unions, especially labour unions, will only consist of non-workers, meaning a union member cannot be working within the plant's premises as a labourer. As such, all union members will be full-time union members and paid to be only so. Management will also provide for full-time union-focused managers, whose sole purpose and job description will be to interface in a positive manner & attitude with the full-time labour & staff union members. The objective of such continuous engagement would always be the betterment of the manufacturing corporation MHTO, across the entire cross section of issues that can be identified and improved upon. Manufacturing stoppages will not be accepted or tolerated, especially if it is due to labour or management issues. All other manufacturing constraints will be duly reported to the appropriate DM, SM & their respective EC. Prompt and adequate solution will be provided without loss of time and productivity.

These DMs, SMs & ECs are adequately equipped with relevant authorities & resources so as to enable smoothening out of any constraints that arise in the manufacture of the H-2-O brand of mineral water, as per pre-identified parameters of quality, quantity & price. As MHTO manufacturing becomes self-sustaining at a saturated equilibrium level, meaning, that full current & future demand is adequately being met or will be, then and only then MHTO can start thinking in terms of the export of H-2-O brand, or as I would prefer, start thinking in terms of making a new pre-identified product(s) which could be added into the Basket of Goods & Services to be supplied to the economic unit after due application & process. Maybe "Thums Up" or "Limca". Or even "100 Plus-an isotonic drink". The manufacturer of which could be invited from another economy!

It's crucial to note that the development of all contemporary economies has been influenced by negotiations between the government, private enterprises, and labor.

In the absence of taxes, prices would decrease by the amount that taxes contribute to the prices of various products, services, and Natural Needs (NN). Incomes would rise by the extent of the tax amounts previously deducted from them. With interest payments for cash deposits in state banks, there is a direct connection between producers and consumers without unnecessary intermediaries. The Decision Makers (DMs), Supply Monitors (SMs), and Economic Coordinators (ECs) are responsible for ensuring this streamlined process.

The impact on the Indian Rupee (INR) would be a strengthening against other currencies and locally, as each INR gains more purchasing power in a PODS economy. However, since most economic units in India don't pay direct taxes, the elimination of taxes could reduce the prices of products and services, potentially leading to increased consumption. Balancing inflation to a minimum or zero would be a challenge for DMs, SMs, and ECs. When it comes to Natural Needs, market interference by these decision-makers is accepted and allowed.

The task ahead for DMs, SMs, and ECs is to efficiently supply all Natural Needs to a population of almost 1.4 billion Indians, a challenging but manageable task given the same population actively participating in manufacturing and production.

23. China It's Mistakes And Lessons

It's worth noting that China has operated in a similar manner to what has been described above since it embraced private enterprise. There are valuable lessons to be learned from both China's mistakes and the positive decisions it has made.

China's Mistakes: One notable mistake was becoming a manufacturing superpower focused on producing the cheapest goods. This led to the construction of industrial infrastructure that prioritized mass production without due consideration for the environment. Even joint venture partners involved in building these factories didn't emphasize environmental concerns. Since compliance costs for environmental standards didn't apply in China, these partners saw cost savings as a significant factor in locating factories there. As China expanded its industrial capabilities, the primary focus was on exports. The belief was that by producing the cheapest product or service, China could dominate the global market for that offering. However, this strategy backfired when consumers, both domestically and internationally, began losing confidence in or interest in the low-quality products China was churning out. Even Chinese consumers started avoiding locally manufactured "lemons." The exported "lemons" found their way mainly to countries with limited production capabilities. Today, the label "Made in China" lacks respect in the international market.

It's interesting how the perception of Chinese products has evolved over time. The shift from desiring Chinese brand products to the attractiveness of "Made for China" indicates the significance of the sheer volume of potential orders associated with the Chinese market.

China's strategy of creating numerous products and services, even if they were inexpensive, led to a surge in consumption. The affordability and appeal of these products induced repeated purchases, contributing to increased consumption. The approach of making products readily available on shelves further fueled consumption patterns.

While China faced challenges related to the reputation of producing "lemons" in the mid-2000s, especially in instances like contaminated toys and milk powders, the remarkable aspect is how the country responded. The decision to shut down polluting factories for the Beijing Olympics, despite potential financial impacts, demonstrates a commitment to environmental concerns. Moreover, the subsequent re-fitting of these factories to meet high pollution and quality standards is a commendable step toward sustainable manufacturing. The ability to manage a vast pool of unemployed labour during this transition period showcases China's adaptability and strategic planning.

The media has always treated China shabbily, and just to show you how, I will provide you with an example:

All factories in China provide dormitories/family dwellings for their labour, that too, near the factory location. Not only that, but special big kitchens dish out a balanced healthy meal for the labour who is so motivated that he or she works long hours. If one can save 2 hours for not cooking & laundry, & another 2 hours by not commuting to & from work, then why not work an extra 4 hours, and that too maybe get paid overtime rates for working these extra 4 hours. Another reason why Chinese labour remains so motivated and disciplined. In China, there are no "sticks" as the media reports: instead, there are real and basic "carrots" that motivate the entire Chinese people. For example, Dormitory accommodation for singles is duly separated by sex type, and even family accommodation neighboring the factory locations.

China also introduced the Prefabricated Concept in infrastructure construction & planning that revolutionized the pace of completing such activities.

Comparatively, in India, despite initiatives like Special Economic Zones (SEZs) and the development of 100 Smart Cities inspired by China, labourers are often left to create makeshift homes near these zones. Unlike China, SEZ developers in India aren't obliged to address the housing needs of labourers.

When China started in 1978 AD, they did not possess a Judiciary system as the one India has. The Judiciary has perhaps done the most damage to India and is easily corrupted by the power of money. When the first bribe was given and taken, the Judiciary should have punished both the giver and the taker of the bribe. But the verdict given was that both were let off. This is because the judiciary has shielded (directly or indirectly) so many corrupt people in all walks of Indian society. Today, the rot is so deep that it will be difficult to stem and eradicate corruption unless extreme drastic steps are taken and executed. Even with so much media attention & hype about corruption, the levels of corruption are still growing, and every now & then "lip service" is provided by the media, whom, is corrupted by the power of money, such that they can go home to their respective homes and pretend that everything is all right and under control. Removing Bottlenecks and quick justice are the call of the day in case the Judiciary wants to clear itself. The Ministry of law should apply to the Ministry of finance for funds that are required to adequately increase the judicial personnel & infrastructure and see the implementation or execution of such judicial delivery systems.

China does not play for or is bothered by The International Arena. If it understands a charge as constructive criticism, it immediately retorts by changing so. Note, China closed 100s of factories so that its Olympic guests could breathe better air, as many observers were noting so.

China runs mainly on the power provided by its ruling class in the manner of an elite group of members who make up The Communist Party of China. Even with a population of more than 1 billion people, there are only 70 million members of the Communist Party of China. There are 56 different ethnic groups. Exclusive schools that train their party personnel in all fields are maintained and run across the country to make them current and future ready. They are the rulers and assume and maintain such positions and empower themselves accordingly.

There is no state religion and not many language diversity obstacles in China. In India, there are hundreds of registered religions, and the constitution is written and recorded in at least 15 languages to date.

Unlike the USA, which has 50 plus states for a population of 400 million & a land area 4 times the land that India consists of; using these numbers and extrapolating, India must gravitate towards forming approximately 200 states and carving these out of the present geography. Pre- Independence, India was a collection of approximately 200 royal states. An interesting coincidence to watch out for is that historical Royals are slowly entering politics. There is nothing wrong with this fragmentation as this would only create & focus on the required administration to govern & manage. Even if they are just DMs, SMs & ECs, in case you have forgotten, by DMs I mean Demand Monitors, by SMs I mean Supply Monitors, and By ECs, I mean Economic Coordinators. The 200 or so sets of state governments would have to entrust themselves to building 200 or so Singapore-type states. More doable this way than it is.

It's crucial to approach information about China with a discerning eye. For instance, in 2008, China's production and consumption of iron and steel amounted to a staggering 550 million metric tons, dwarfing India's 50 million metric tons during the same period. In 2008 AD, it was reported that China supposedly grew at 9 % while India was at 7%.

This was reported, but if you look at these actual figures for Iron & Steel production & consumption, you wonder what is being reported, and what the objective of this kind of reporting is all about.

24. A Pods Example- Macro And Micro

Starting with a premise, it's crucial to highlight that in a tax-less economy, the government, or banks, by not imposing taxes, liberate themselves from direct accountability to the taxpayers. This departure from the traditional taxation model allows them greater flexibility in expenditure, fostering a more distributed approach. It's essential to note that the concept of taxation is inherently tied to monarchies and not inherently democratic, given its non-voluntary nature.

Assumption: There are no delays in supply, production, or execution. Additionally, a robust digital, computer-driven electronic infrastructure is in place, manned by honest and well-compensated personnel across various job categories. As an illustration, let's consider the construction of a 50 km road equipped with self-driven car technology embedded in the infrastructure. Assuming that, after thorough evaluation, the cost of building this road is estimated to be 500 crores (One crore=10 million), the Ministry of Transport submits a proposal to the Ministry of Finance (MoF). The MoF assigns a team of professionals, including CPAs/CAs, cost accountants, commerce, and economic graduates (with tax officials assuming roles as auditors), civil and road engineers, etc., to monitor, audit, and execute the project in real-time.

Upon approval, the MoF directs the Reserve Bank of India (RBI) to issue an electronic credit of 500 crores to the Reserve Bank of India (RBI) Account specifically designated for the 50 km road project (RBI50KM). An authorized RBI official inputs the amount of 500 crores into the RBI's NEFT/RTGS/OTHER ELECTRONIC PLATFORM computer system, and the electronic credit is seamlessly transferred to the State Bank of India (SBI) 50KM account.

The SBI bank account officials in consultation & knowledge of the project contractor further disperse the monies electronically into the various accounts of vendors, contractors, and material & equipment suppliers as well as to management, staff & labour. Similarly, another 500 crores are also issued to the manufacturers of materials & equipment that will be utilized in making this road, as well as issued to the manufacturers and producers of the entire basket of goods, products & services consumed by all the personnel attached to this project. At the end of the project, the 500 (demand side) + 500 (supply side) = 1000 crores (Balanced deficit) will be backed by a 50 KM road asset, and experienced personnel who worked in different capacities to construct the roadway, & not by manner of equivalent bullion, or any basket of currency values, treasury bills or bonds. Part of the 500 crores issued to the suppliers of the consumables to personnel of the contractor, raw material, and equipment suppliers will be returned as these consumables are paid for by the personnel via their digital salaries. So, the second tranche of 500 crores will act as an advance to the manufacturers and producers of consumables, whereby zero percent loans issued to these producers will be paid back or adjusted as PLI's. To explain further, 500 crores of the 1000 crore asset will. The officials at the State Bank of India (SBI), in collaboration with the project contractor, electronically disburse the funds to various accounts, including vendors, contractors, material and equipment suppliers, as well as management, staff, and labor involved in the project. Similarly, another 500 crores are issued to the manufacturers of materials and equipment used in constructing the road, as well as to the producers of the entire array of goods, products, and services consumed by all personnel associated with the project.

By the end of the project, the 500 crores issued on the demand side, plus the 500 crores issued on the supply side, totaling 1000 crores (a balanced deficit), will be backed by the asset of a 50 km road and the experienced personnel who contributed to its construction. This backing is not in the form of equivalent bullion, currency values, treasury bills, or bonds but rather the tangible asset created.

Part of the 500 crores issued to suppliers of consumables to project personnel, raw materials, and equipment suppliers will be returned as these consumables are paid for by the personnel through their digital salaries. Therefore, the second tranche of 500 crores serves as an advance to the manufacturers and producers of consumables. This creates a cycle where the funds lent to producers are paid back or adjusted as PLIs.

To elaborate further, 500 crores of the 1000 crore asset will be inherent in the quantity and quality of personnel who built the project, as they consumed what they earned. This, in turn, circulates back to the bank through the vendors of consumables who have been provided with loans by the bank (at zero interest to produce the consumed items), subject to any effective PLIs.

This example can be replicated for various projects, as long as one unit of electronic money demanded is backed by one unit of actual physical supplies, made available for consumption. There is no limit on the money demanded if a balanced deficit is supported by project-executed assets, and manufactured and supplied goods, products, and services are consistently delivered. The liabilities of wages, costs, and expenses of resources are matched by the asset of a 50 km smart roadway and the "consumed personnel". As 500 crore was issued both to the producers' side and consumption side, any sales revenues to the producer will be returned to the bank to maintain financial discipline.

The process of generating money electronically through platforms like NEFT, RTGS, or other electronic means can eliminate the need for taxes. With the Reserve Bank of India (RBI) and State Bank of India (SBI) being part of the government, the issuance of money for various projects can be managed through such electronic methods. It is crucial, however, to establish robust checks and balances on systems and authorized personnel to ensure the responsible issuance of money in this manner.

In the absence of taxes, all money circulating in the economy would be considered "white," eliminating the need for individuals and businesses to engage in speculative markets to earn from their capital. Deposits in the banking system could earn interest at a rate of 10%, tax-free as an electronic credit. The guarantee of 100% deposit and interest protection applies if these balances are digitally transacted and not used for speculative purposes. This shift would streamline the economic process by removing layers of speculators between producers and consumers, potentially leading to deflation. While prices decrease, real income would increase, with wages either remaining the same or even rising.

The removal of taxes would also necessitate the mandatory banking of all cash, which becomes more feasible in a tax-free environment. Electronic credits could be issued based on deposits to facilitate transactions in a cashless economy, without the need for new issues of physical currency. However, stringent measures must be in place to ensure the accuracy and security of electronic currency transactions, guarding against errors or fraud. The transition to a cashless and tax-less economy requires careful planning, execution, and education for the entire population to participate seamlessly.

Awarding government tenders based on the most value for money rather than the lowest bid is crucial. The emphasis should be on T1 (Best Technology Bid), as the best technology cannot be compromised at the cost of the lowest price. It's essential to accompany tenders with thorough Decision Tree analysis and Critical Path Method (CPM) analysis, with a legal commitment to execute and complete the project as presented.

Contractors and vendors must receive adequate funds to execute projects, and any failure to fulfill committed obligations should be met with strict punishment and liability. This approach is vital to prevent inflation and ensure the success of the entire project.

The Government of India (GOI) should adopt a stance of "maximizing balanced deficits" in alignment with the PODS banking paradigm. This strategy focuses on optimizing deficits in a balanced manner, promoting economic stability and efficient resource allocation.

Now to a microeconomic example:

let's consider purchasing 250 grams of tea bags for your morning cup. Today, with numerous online platforms, you have the flexibility to explore various brands and qualities, make a digital payment, and receive your chosen tea within a few hours or up to a day. The delivery time is crucial, designed to be so short that it prevents inflation or deflation between the pre-order payment and delivery. Real-time monitoring by web portals allows them to inform tea vendors of sales trends, enabling vendors to adjust their stocks, anticipate demand for specific brands, and ensure that your preferred 250 grams of "X" tea brand is ready for delivery based on your typical buying pattern.

25. Suggested Changeover Process

In the transition from the current macro and microeconomic systems to the PODS system, all citizens' money will need to be deposited in banks, and the interest rate on these legitimate cash deposits will be set at a tax-free 10 percent. Those who have been paying taxes will receive their due payments, with a tax-free 10% interest per annum added to the taxed amounts as capital balances, along with an inflation adjustment.

To facilitate this transition, the establishment of a Domestic Global Bank may be considered, specifically for the purpose of moving from the existing Grey economy to the Green economy— let's call it THE GLOBAL CHANGEOVER BANK (TGCB). This bank would operate in a way that allows each economy to fund its changeover requirements using its own currency deficits and bridge currency loans from TGCB, which could be in another relevant economy's currency or currencies. These funds could be utilized for developing or expediting technology acquisition to facilitate the transition. TGCB would play a crucial role in financing the shift from existing Grey economic capacities to Green economic capacities, with a focus on achieving a 100% Green economy. No profits would be allowed in this process. The experience gained during and after the Greening process would then inform further actions and decisions.

26. Health And Police/Judiciary Under Pods

Health and the Judiciary will primarily be in the government sector. The rationale is that a Doctor of Medicine, to sustain a living, might subconsciously expect or imply, "someone gets unwell" to earn a livelihood, while a lawyer might need to think or imply/expect, "someone please commit a crime" to make a living. Pharmaceuticals and other branches of medicine often depend on people becoming sick and may not be profitable without indirectly encouraging disease. Bringing these sectors into the government or a joint private-government sector could address these issues. However, as the government now procures the best services, a comprehensive compensation system would need to be developed for doctors and lawyers based on their abilities, with higher compensation for the more skilled professionals compared to others. Hospitals and courts would receive more compensation when they have fewer cases, incentivizing efficiency over quantity. Doctors and lawyers would also be compensated when they don't have work, encouraging them to engage in hospital or court management, focusing on research and development in their respective fields, activities that would be adequately funded.

Civil defense or civil crime can result from incorrect economics, making the implementation and nurturing of PODS even more crucial. As an example, consider an Indian citizen whose father is seriously ill, and the doctors require 125,000 rupees for treatment, an amount beyond the financial reach of the citizen, and the illness is life-threatening.

What should or can a citizen do?

Borrowing money in this situation presents a few options: seeking assistance from a relative or friend, approaching a money lender, or turning to a bank. However, relatives and friends may not have the necessary funds, and dealing with a money lender could involve exorbitant demands, such as personal favours or unreasonable returns, as illustrated by the example where the money lender seeks time with the citizen's wife as interest. Turning to a bank is a viable option, but the bureaucratic process typically takes two weeks, which is not conducive to the immediate financial needs of the citizen.

In this scenario, the citizen, desperate to save his father's life, resorts to stealing from the money lender. Despite successfully obtaining the funds needed for his father's treatment, he is apprehended and sentenced to a two-year jail term. As the sole provider for his family, his incarceration leaves his father and the family without support. Tragically, by the time he is released, his father succumbs to the lack of prescribed medicines.

This example, though not to be personally identified with, serves to illustrate the harsh consequences individuals may face in desperate situations. In the proposed PODS model, where health is a state responsibility, the citizen's father would have received timely and cost-free treatment. While it would have incurred some economic effort for the state, the positive outcomes, such as preventing a productive citizen from turning to crime and ensuring a long and healthy life for a senior citizen, highlight the potential benefits of effective economic planning in addressing factors that contribute to civil or economic crime.

In the proposed PODS model, Judicial and Health Services will be provided on a First Come First Served Basis, with an option for individuals to voluntarily buy a position in line. While planning for future medical capacities, provisions may include the creation of DNA banks or Stem Cell banks to address medical bottlenecks, especially for elders. To ensure efficient use of deceased individuals, an alternative to full cremation is suggested, encouraging the use of salvageable body parts. Biological heirs can be compensated for the harvested parts, with measures in place to prevent premature and intentional creation of death for organ harvesting. Additionally, the concept of standing graves is proposed to save land space traditionally used for tombs, reducing it from two yards to one yard. To enhance judicial capacities, immediate empowerment of bureaucrats and police can be considered, followed by ongoing estimations and adjustments to meet day-to-day functioning needs after addressing any backlog.

27. Agriculture, Food, And Education

Once the Judiciary and Health functions are smoothly operational, the focus will shift to financing and implementing free food and education initiatives.

For Food and Education, the economic unit will be the Village, and all cultivated land will be managed by the elected Panchayat (Village Governance Council). The land allocation will consider factors such as fertility and other relevant criteria, quantifying each villager's numeric percentage value in the village's agricultural output. Villagers without land, even if holding Benami (proxy-owned) land, will be covered by the Village Panchayat, ensuring free food, a supervised unemployed allowance in digital cash and kind, and employment opportunities if desired. Unlanded villagers can run Village Kitchens, with one of them holding a compulsory position in the Panchayat for reporting adherence to proper treatment of the unlanded poor to PODS village authorities.

Benami Landlords will maintain land ownership, with updated records reflecting actual holdings based on a cut-off date. Calculation of what a landlord is allowed to own will involve contributions to the "actual unlanded personnel fund" equitably based on agricultural output and village population figures. This contribution can be fulfilled through sustainable employment in agricultural or other economic activities on the village farm. Initially, agricultural output, including livestock, will drive and identify village economic output, gradually expanding to include other economic activities like cottage and handicraft items. Education infrastructure will be aligned with the population and demographics, and necessary capital and variable funds will be digitally deposited directly into the Village Bank Account. All educational accessories including stationary, smartphones, notebooks and tablets, textbooks (access to E-Libraries) & uniforms whenever students must meet offline, will be provided by the State only in physical form. Most importantly, teachers would also be treated on par with doctors & lawyers, and similar hierarchy and compensation systems based on abilities would also be put in place. All educational institutions and teachers will be ranked in a comparable manner. Teachers of a particular rank will be funded to teach only those that they want to teach and will be allowed to be independent of institutions if they choose to do so.

Educational content should undergo a radical reevaluation, prioritizing practical knowledge relevant to real life. Questions like the usefulness of Algebra or Trigonometry in everyday situations are raised, emphasizing the need for education to focus on life skills such as table manners, basic politeness, personal care, laundry, and cooking.

The conventional approach of exams and tests, often featuring questions with limited real-life applicability, is challenged. Instead, the proposal suggests a shift towards assessing students based on what they have genuinely learned from a subject or chapter. This approach not only encourages a deeper understanding but also serves as an automatic audit on the effectiveness of teaching methods, making both teachers and education authorities accountable.

The question is posed: Should education be about nurturing out-of-the-box thinkers and those who ask questions, or is it merely a process of producing human robots who conform to a set routine?

The essence of education, whether seen as a full-time job or a service, is pondered, extending the reflection to include sports education as well.

The Covid-19 pandemic highlighted the viability of remote education, emphasizing the potential of learning from home or any connected location with efficient internet access. The prevalence of E-books and E-libraries, some of which are free, while others require subscription, is transforming education, making quality learning accessible worldwide. Top universities now offer online classes with valid certificates and degrees, mirroring the increasing popularity and affordability of online education, demonstrated by the multitude of online school classes and tuitions.

Rather than traditional exams, a proposed approach involves students writing email messages to their teachers after each class, expressing what they have learned. This ongoing communication allows teachers to assess students' understanding, provide corrections, guidance, and suggest additional readings. For higher degrees and certificates, supervised qualification and aptitude tests could be implemented. The choice between physical and online learning is presented as a flexible option based on individual capacities.

This model keeps both teachers and students engaged, eliminating absenteeism, and allows for self-directed learning akin to Eklavya's journey with an imaginary Guru. The shift to digital learning reduces environmental impact by eliminating the need for paper, pencils, and ink. The funds that would have been spent on traditional books can now be redirected to acquiring solar- powered smartphones, tablets, and laptops, along with subscriptions to digital libraries aligned with the school or college curriculum.

This flexible and accessible education system, coupled with economic models like Planned & Organized Deficit Spending (PODS), has the potential to create a peaceful and prosperous world with diverse economies meeting basic standards. With PODS, education is viewed as a job, reinforcing the idea that a planet with universal education can lead to overall prosperity and development.

28. Pods Now, Why Not Earlier?

The concept of Planned & Organized Deficit Spending (PODS) wasn't envisioned in the early days of economic thought due to the predominant reliance on tax collection setups as major job and service providers in every country or economy. Shifting from traditional tax collectors and enforcers to becoming both Demand and Supply Monitors (DM & SM) and Economic Coordinators (EC) involves a challenging transition for the existing personnel infrastructure.

Under PODS, the entire personnel structure of tax collection transforms into Demand and Supply Channel Monitors. Each product or service pre-identified by the Economic-Administrative Committee (EAC) has dedicated Demand Monitors who assess and report the demand, while Supply Monitors ensure that the assessed demand is met through actual supply. The Economic Coordinators facilitate coordination between Demand and Supply Monitors to achieve targeted demand-supply equilibrium up to market saturation or total sustainable equilibrium for the chosen products and services.

The monies required for this system are the Allowable Deficit, enforced by supplying until a distributed equilibrium of matching supply and demand is achieved in the economy. Economic Coordinators also serve as real-time auditors, ensuring that production and consumption are in alignment, and overall equilibrium is maintained. This represents a significant departure from traditional tax-focused economic models.

Economic Coordinators will also act as real-time auditors, making sure that production & consumption match.

29. Note On Pods Versus Foreign Direct Investment (Fdi) Route

In the PODS model, even with the assumption of a supply lag and an electro-digital infrastructure, financing projects through Foreign Direct Investment (FDI) would not be the most cost-effective route. If FDI were chosen, the Central Bank of the Economy would receive the foreign investment, which would then be converted into the local currency and introduced into the system for the specific project.

For instance, consider the Vedanta Group's joint venture with the Foxconn Group, bringing in 20 billion USD as FDI for a chip manufacturing project in India. This FDI would translate to approximately 1600 billion rupees once converted. In this scenario, a 20-billion-dollar project would result in the issuance of an additional 1600 billion rupees, potentially causing a global inflation impact. Moreover, there would be an outflow when initial capital and profits are repatriated back to the FDI economy.

An alternative proposal suggests bypassing the FDI route and directly approaching the local Central bank to fund the project, eliminating the need for foreign conversion, and mitigating potential inflationary consequences.

In the PODS model, instead of opting for the Foreign Direct Investment (FDI) route, the government could instruct local banks, such as the State Bank of India, to provide an adequate interest-free line of credit to companies like Mercedes for specific projects, such as manufacturing "Zero Emission Cars" in India. This approach eliminates the need for foreign conversion and potential outflows associated with FDI. The government can offer incentives such as land, power, and access to well-educated personnel to make the invitation more attractive.

Bona-fide loans to priority sectors, including local and domestic production capacities, could be interest-free. Furthermore, funds or loans to priority sectors might come with additional monetary benefits, acting as a rebate or inflow for the recipient. The rate of this rebate or inflow could vary based on the priority level of the product, service, or sector. Priority would be determined by the economic importance of the product or service in question.

To offset bank risk concerns, manufacturers and producers would be responsible for execution and operational risks, which could be insured. The savings generated from the absence of interest costs on capital and working capital could be passed on to labour in the form of higher wages. This, in turn, enhances the purchasing capacity of the labour force, contributing to improved living standards. The increased productivity resulting from directing interest savings into better working conditions and environments would contribute to the overall competitiveness of the industry.

It should be compulsory for FDI to come in kinds like equipment and machinery and not in CBDC. Whatever expenditure will be incurred in domestic economy that sum of domestic CBDC will be issued in the local economy.

30. Insurance In Pods And Non-Pods, Real-World Insurance Suggestions

Public sector insurance companies offer coverage for business execution and operations risks. This could be a mutually beneficial arrangement, where businesses receive coverage for their specific risks, and the insurance companies, being public sector entities, contribute to maintaining a healthy business environment.

For instance, consider a manufacturer of Rubber Rolls supplying Rice Mills. If the State Electricity Board (S.E.B) provides electricity at INR 5 per unit, and in case of a power failure, the manufacturer must resort to a generator at a cost of INR 12 per unit, an insurance policy could compensate for the difference of INR 7 per unit.

This kind of policy not only safeguards the business against financial losses but also acts as a check on the S.E.B. The public sector insurance company, by providing such coverage, incentivizes the

S.E.B to improve its services since any compensation would need to be paid by the S.E.B to the insurance company. It creates a mechanism for accountability and improvement in the public services.

Furthermore, policies covering EMIs in case of income loss could also be considered. If an individual paying an EMI loses their source of income due to acceptable reasons, the insurance policy would come into play, providing a safety net for such individuals, and ensuring financial stability during challenging times. This approach aligns with the idea of social responsibility and support within the economic framework.

Another policy consideration could involve covering risks associated with speculative activities in the stock equity market and other speculative business endeavours.

On the topic of hedging and foreign exchange risks, the idea of fixing currency rates across states could simplify transactions and remove the need for complex hedging mechanisms. If every state economy operates with a fixed exchange rate, it eliminates the uncertainty associated with currency fluctuations and reduces the costs incurred in brokerage for foreign exchange transactions. The proposal to establish casinos at the local level, managed through public or government sector banks, offers an intriguing alternative. With this setup, individuals would have the opportunity to engage in speculative activities within a controlled environment. The presence of public sector banks could ensure responsible gambling practices, preventing individuals from incurring significant losses. However, it's essential to strike a balance to prevent excessive reliance on such activities and maintain a productive society.

31. To Export, Or Add Another Pre-Identified Product Or Service

Once the PODS economy reaches a point where the demand and supply for pre-identified products or services are in sustainable equilibrium and the markets are fully saturated, it can then be considered transitioning into a "Latest Model" market economy (LME). At this stage, if the economy wishes to do so, it can explore the option of exporting its surplus products or services. This strategic move ensures that the domestic needs are well-met before engaging in international trade, contributing to a stable and self-sufficient economic model.

It's often more prudent for an economy to focus on maintaining a balance in the demand and supply equation and expanding the variety of pre-identified products or services within the domestic market rather than aggressively pursuing exports. Japan's approach in the mid-1970s, where it first saturated its domestic demand before entering international markets with products like Toyota cars, serves as a noteworthy example. In the current economic landscape of individual states, prioritizing equilibrium and diversification within the local market could be a more sustainable and beneficial strategy. It's interesting to note that Japan has successfully implemented a progressive welfare economy, emphasizing the government's responsibility for the well-being of its citizens throughout their lives, guided by a benevolent Emperor and politicians.

32. Pods And Foreign Exchange-Hard Currencies

Managing hard currency requirements for crucial sectors like Energy and Defense, or for accessing "Technology Short Cuts," can indeed be a complex task. Financing options include generating revenue through exports to hard currency economies or providing zero-interest loans from the Central Bank to technology providers. In the case of technology development, the government can allocate funds for in-house research and development, ensuring self-sufficiency in critical technologies over time. Additionally, exploring innovative approaches, such as taxing Non- Resident Citizens living in the required currency economy, can generate substantial funds. For instance, implementing a reasonable tax on Non-Resident Indians (NRIs) could contribute significantly to meeting hard currency needs, offering a potential annual revenue source.

It is to be observed that even after 70 years of self-rule, the statistics, or data available to policymakers in India are based on statistical methods of guessing and probabilities. Even now, economic policy direction and reporting are just guesses from people (not to belittle them) who have developed a "gut feel" over years of working with data that are estimates or educated guesses. Accurate and real-time data is crucial for effective policymaking and economic planning. The Gati Shakti and PLI schemes in India are indeed significant steps toward enhancing data collection and analysis. It's essential to move away from relying on estimates and guesses, shifting towards a data-driven approach to better understand and address economic challenges. Developing a comprehensive and precise data infrastructure will empower policymakers with the insights needed to make informed decisions and shape effective strategies for economic development.

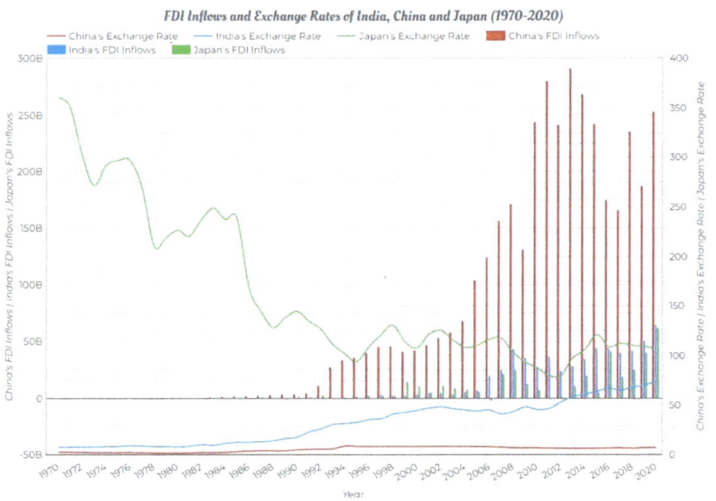

Figure 6: FDI Inflows and Exchange Rates of India, China and Japan (1970-2020)

This Chart graphs the FDI and Exchange Rates of India, China and Japan between 1970-2020. This data is sourced from the World Bank.

China: China's success in maintaining a stable foreign exchange rate over several decades played a crucial role in attracting foreign direct investment (FDI) and fostering a conducive economic environment. The stability in currency and economic conditions instilled confidence in investors, creating a solid foundation for business operations. This, coupled with a high level of trust and the absence of concerns about returns on investment, encouraged significant inflows of FDI, capital expenditure (CAPEX), and advanced technology. China's universities, research and development initiatives, and industrial units further contributed to its economic growth, ultimately improving the standard of living for its citizens.

India: India faced challenges in attracting significant foreign direct investment (FDI) despite economic liberalization in 1991. The graph indicates that FDI started to increase around 2004- 2005. The depreciation of the currency over time presented obstacles in creating an attractive platform for investment in both capital expenditure (CAPEX) and technology (TECHEX). The continuous depreciation also contributed to apprehensions among FDI investors, limiting India's bargaining power to attract substantial CAPEX, TECHTEX, and FDI.

Additionally, India lacked a robust chain of knowledge integration between universities, research and development, and industry. This absence hindered the country from gaining a competitive advantage and bargaining power to engage in commerce on mutually beneficial terms.

Japan: Japan, following World War II, was mandated to focus on producing goods, services, and agriculture for peaceful purposes only. Having developed industrial capacity during both World War I and II, Japan operated largely through self-financing after the war. Notably, Japan's commerce relied on in-house developed technology, and throughout the period from 1970 to 2020, foreign direct investment (FDI) inflows were minimal. Japan prioritized supplying its domestic economy before considering the export of surpluses. For instance, Suzuki cars did not gain international recognition until the 1970s-75s.

China's remarkable growth since 2004-5 can be attributed significantly to a stable currency. Even with the opening of their stock markets and allowing foreign capital to trade in equity, China maintained a stable fixed currency, fostering an environment conducive to growth.

Comparing India and Japan, Japan, despite being a superior economic power, has more domestic currency units (Yen) per USD compared to the INR per USD.

In terms of population, the USA with 400 million and Japan with 120 million can be compared on an equal footing with similar-sized populations. Interestingly, the top 120 million people in India could be considered at par with the entire Japanese population.

33. Pods In India; Foreign Firms And Fx

Mr. Agarwal's (Vedanta Resources) suggestion for India to remain a consuming market is welcomed, with the condition that all imports are paid in digital E-currency. In a fully digital economy, foreign exchange rates may become unpredictable, requiring caution from sovereign/digital currency issuers. The Indian economy can function as a free market as long as goods are imported and sold through the payment of domestic E-currency. Foreign companies, even if not on the Invitation/Preferred List, are welcome to set up operations in the PODS economy and enjoy its benefits. For a foreign company to manufacture a product or provide a service in this economy, it should fall into a pre-identified category or qualify as a luxury offering. If the company has a critical, relevant, or future-ready product or service, it can apply for an invitation. If it chooses not to apply or declines an invitation but is deemed critical, relevant, or future-ready, setting up an R & D operation may be encouraged to develop the required technology. Efforts can be made to attract the company or technocrats to establish a presence in PODS INDIA.

Foreign companies, whether wholly or partly owned, when invited and granted a line of credit by a Local Central Bank or its branch, may have their technical and financial credentials endorsed and guaranteed by their own domestic central bank and relevant government departments. This guaranteed requirement, though not mandatory, could be implemented to safeguard against scenarios like DAEWOO or ENRON. If these foreign entities choose to remit profits to their home economies, a tax of 110% will be imposed on the remitted amount, with the net 10% to be received in the physical real currency of the recipient economy. If profits and capital are retained within the India-Indian PODS economy, deposit and interest payments will be 100% guaranteed, provided the funds are spent digitally and not for speculative purposes. This allows for the holding of Indian Rupees by foreign corporations or governments, not out of economic necessity for India but because of the PODS model.

In a system without taxes, commerce would operate on a "No Profit No Loss" basis. This approach considers a facet of capitalism that is often overlooked—organizing allowable deficits in a manner that, if physical demand and supply match, targets the actual and physical manufacture and supply of all pre-identified products/services in a sustainable and all-encompassing manner. The goal is to strive for a distributed equilibrium in the relevant products/services market, at least in the context of PODS India. Corporates, whether private, joint sector, or government, should be allowed to directly engage with their respective Central banks for funding requirements. In the current profit-maximizing mode of capitalism, embracing a "no profit no loss" stance provides an alternative. Both capitalism and communism need to humanize their approaches and are currently irrelevant spending forces. Encouraging the public sector, especially in India, to act as a regulator on private sector excesses or shortcomings within the same industry is crucial. Simultaneously, the private sector acts as a check on public sector corporations in the same sector. The financial landscape has witnessed a shift in recent years, with many financial professionals who once earned substantial pay checks and bonuses falling out of favour. The emergence of newcomers in the realms of the Bulls and the Bears is now a rare occurrence. While a bear can consume a bull in the real world, the reverse is not a common occurrence. Investors, accustomed to high returns, contribute to the volatility observed in equity markets and commodities.

In commodities markets, the prevalence of futures trading lacks a check on the proportion of paper lots traded compared to actual physical lots. The concept of hedging is often advocated to mitigate risks in commodities or currencies. However, an alternative approach could involve fixing the prices of commodities and currencies. Any potential losses in earnings from fixed prices could be compensated by holding corporate equity, which could earn more. Alternatively, if equity is converted to debt, as mentioned earlier, it allows for pre-accounting in a more known and stable business environment.

The CEO of a prominent international bank recently called for bankers and similar professionals responsible for the economic turmoil since 2008 to publicly apologize for their mistakes. However, in response to this, credit card holders and individuals who have made purchases on credit are also expressing a desire to apologize. They are urging the CEO to consider writing off their debts, especially considering the current job losses they are facing, while the CEO, as a banker, retains job security. I've always found banking a bit perplexing. For instance, take LIBOR, now replaced with the US$ SOFR (Secured Overnight Financing Rate), currently at 2.96%—why collect deposits from the public and offer them more than LIBOR/SOFR? The same confusion applies to SIBOR, and now there's even IBOR. In India, the Reserve Bank of India lends to banks at a rate of 6.25%, while banks are soliciting deposits from the public at rates ranging from 6-7% upwards, only to lend them out at a minimum of 11% per annum. Maybe my understanding is wrong, but it seems like there's a considerable spread between deposit and lending rates in India, ranging from 4-9%, making banking, even in the public/government sector, profitable despite potential hidden non-performing assets (NPAs). Banks in the USA were operating with a gross spread between deposit and lending rates of less than 0.50%-1%. It seems likely that U.S. banks with international branches, including those in India, earned enough to subsidize their domestic operations. A case in point is Citibank, which, despite facing challenges domestically, maintains a robust presence in India. This phenomenon raises questions about how the survival of branches is sustained when the headquarters may be facing financial difficulties. The narrow spreads between deposit and lending rates were a significant contributing factor to the 2008 economic crisis. With thin spreads, banks had to channel funds into investments with higher returns to cover costs.

The financial crisis of 2008 unfolded as investment bankers leveraged bank deposits with low- interest earnings to engage in high-risk activities in the equity and commodity markets. These activities brought in substantial returns, significantly contributing to the banks' profits. However, the bankers failed to realize that once the investment bankers received their hefty bonuses and pay checks, they were no longer responsible for market fluctuations.

The assumption was that the market would remain bullish, but increasing volatility and substantial daily gains or losses made the risks more pronounced. Traders and brokerages could make enormous profits or losses based on market movements, leading to a situation where a few wrong positions could collapse the entire system. While such cycles had occurred in the past and were corrected, the scale of the 2008 crisis was unprecedented, making it challenging to recover.

In the context of Planned and Organized Deficit Spending (PODS), the pain of utilizing taxpayers' funds to address such crises could be alleviated, providing a more effective mechanism for regulating and fixing economic challenges. The attractiveness and viability of decoupling the world economy from the Dollar and Pound currencies are growing. The Eurozone, if it repeats the same mistakes, might lose its original purpose, and could better serve by not accommodating the US dollar and British Pound, allowing their true unaccommodated lower values to be reflected.

The remaining buoyancy of the US Dollar relies on the fact that over 70% of the global crude petroleum and by-products trade is conducted in US Dollars. However, there is growing discontent on both the producer and consumer sides, advocating for the use of direct currencies in crude oil transactions instead of exclusively relying on the US Dollar. For instance, India could pay for its significant crude petroleum imports in Indian Rupees (INR), and the producers could then use the INR for buying out of India or spending in India.

Diversifying the currencies used for crude petroleum and by-products imports makes sense, ensuring a well-balanced and diversified portfolio for the producer economies. It aligns with the fundamental finance principle of diversification, even in the realm of currencies.

Before transitioning to this approach, it would be wise for oil-producing nations to permanently fix their respective currency values with the US Dollar, British Pound, and Euro. This strategy ensures that their reserves in these currencies maintain a steady and known fixed value, assuming that there is no desired appreciation in these currencies.

PODS is applicable not only to underdeveloped and developing economies but has been tested in developed economies as well. Through total computerization, PODS allows accurate calculations of demand and supply. It assures that no economy is overly dependent on another, and each economy is accountable for its own success or failure. With PODS in place, there are fewer excuses for economic failures, and every economy has the potential to achieve a stand-alone status in NN capabilities over time.

Moving towards a Global Entity after achieving self-sufficiency through PODS is a logical progression. In this economic society, individual economic units cannot blame the overall economic situation for their failures or weaknesses. With no money or capital constraints in PODS, there are no excuses for economic failures, and accountability rests with the economic unit personnel.

The notion that what is manufactured as a product or service in any economy represents the "ounce of gold" behind that economy's currency is a powerful concept. The traditional Gold Standard for currency valuation was abandoned by major economies in 1971 AD.

To address economic challenges, even a vibrant and economically sound entity like Dubai could introduce innovative solutions. For example, the Dubai government could implement an 'economic failure tax' (EFT) of USD 3000 per ex-pat worker annually, potentially raising USD 10.5 billion from its 3.5 million ex-pat workers. This EFT could be a temporary measure, to be returned once the Dubai economy regains stability. It's a unique approach considering Dubai's usual tax-free status.

34. Smart City & Other Project Land Procurement: Strategy & Suggested Process/Procedures

To initiate the procurement of land for significant projects such as smart cities and industrial developments, the relevant Land and Development Office (L&DO) can issue a notice or tender to all Panchayats in the state or country.

For Example:

Suggested Notice/Tender Content:

"Appeal to villages in West Bengal: Requested 30,000 acres in one contiguous lot required by an internationally known Indian steel company for their intention to set up a 5 million MT Iron & Steel plant besides other ancillary units. Land should be located near rivers, roads, railway tracks, environmentally clean power stations, and iron ore mines. An additional 1000 acres may be required for setting up a power plant that will be of the highest international technological standard, environmentally clean & green. It is preferred that this should be near a coal mine. This will be converted into a smart city with the steel industry being its specialization.

The land acquisition process will adhere to the following guidelines:

1. Housing Development: Prior to any physical possession of the required land, properly improved and environmentally friendly dwelling units will be constructed at the perimeters of the land parcel for the displaced individuals or families.
2. Income Assessment: The income of each displaced unit, whether individual or family, will be assessed based on their previous land usage. This includes both in-kind (grains, vegetables, fruits) and cash generated from the sale of produce or livestock.
3. Compensation: The land buyer/receiver will provide compensation, in cash and kind, equivalent to the assessed income as soon as displacement is affected and the settled are given possession of their new dwellings. Once the project is commissioned, additional compensation, accounted as dividends, will be provided. In the case of no profit, this will be treated as a liability with a minimum pre-fixed dividend.
4. Equity Issuance: Original landowners will be issued non-transferable equity in the new entity, entitled to normal earnings over and above the "Special Class" equity holders.
5. Job Opportunities: One or more job opportunities per household displaced will be offered without any reduction in cash and kind amounts.
6. Skills Development: Vocational training and skills development will be provided to support smart city requirements. Micro-credit may be extended to displaced individuals or families for establishing support facilities for the smart city.

7. Commercial Opportunities: Displaced individuals or families may engage in commercial activities, such as supplying fresh vegetables, fruits, poultry, milk, and milk products to the project personnel in a professionally organized or cooperative manner.
8. Loan Repayment: If the land of the displaced unit is mortgaged, the outstanding loan balance just prior to possession must be fully repaid to transfer the land to the new owner with a clear title.

Note: Any tax implications on the displaced unit will be borne by the new landowner. The compensation amounts can be offset by government grants or tax deductions to the project firm, and CSR budgets may also contribute to these expenses. Special care will be taken to prevent any mischief in the case of mortgaged lands.

Upon receiving the notice/tender, villages that meet the requirements as per the above-mentioned parameters will decide amongst themselves, whether they would be willing to “give” their land in a manner as is described in the notice/tender; and thereafter, having decided to volunteer their lands would engage the relevant government machinery/ department entity via its Panchayats (especially so, in these times of Panchayati Raj), or legal representative(s), to begin the process of the relevant land transfer to the would-be buyer of the entire 31,000 acres.

To start the process instead of fencing the land which would be exchanged by the villagers as a result of this engagement between the village and the land buyer via the government land department, it would be better if one laid the foundation stone for the dwelling units which would replace the displaced people’s original dwelling units and build this building(s) first.

Once people see this building(s) come up, and these surveys (re consumption/ production...cash & kind payments, etc.) executed or intended to be executed, automatically; the entire targeted amount of land should become available. Landowners will come to the buyer of the land via the government land department (L&DO), instead of playing an "unfair game" with existing landowners and making the state fight its own citizens by making the state dispossess its citizens of their lands without proper and fair compensation. I assume you would agree that if the land was possessed as per the above manner of compensation, you would agree that the compensation offered for land is fair and adequate. It is to be noted that landowners have been using their land for ages and eking a livelihood, however good or bad it was, and as the families grew in terms of family members, the earnings were diluted. Just paying cash to these landowners who normally are not that money savvy would drive those to spend the monies so received, and thereafter, they would be landless as well as penniless. This may drive them to crime or other untoward activities which would degrade the smart city. If the land exchanges hands in the suggested manner there also will be no regrets about being dispossessed of the land by the original landowners in the future.

If the land is taken over in the manner described, then the landowner will get a steady income from his/her ancestral lands and will continuously do so for generations to come also.

If no one responds to the notice/tender, it would be best that NO land is allocated for the subject project in West Bengal & an alternate state located in the country be considered in the same manner.

NOTE: This is just an example only.

It would be advisable to put students who have topped their degrees and chosen from across universities and engineering schools from across India to form a team which would lead in making and planning each of the 100 (280) smart cities, dedicated and specialized to one or more economic activity. It would be like building 280 Singapore or Dubai city states across India. This is the task that is required of all the citizens of Bharath.

Each of these city areas must be self-sufficient in Food & Agriculture, Water & Green Electricity.

Salaries and wages for all personnel working in these smart cities must be comparable to any if not all foreign destinations for employment.

35. Agriculture India-For The Farmer-Big Or Small- One Village One Farm

There are 664,369 villages in India as of 2020. Out of these inhabited villages in the country, the largest number of villages (145,000) is in the population (See Figure A below) size group of 500- 999 persons, followed by the groups 100-1999 (130,000) and 200-499 (128,000). There are 3,961 villages, which have a population of 10,000 persons or more.

India's Population & Distribution of Villages/clusters:

Many population clusters, due to the different qualification definitions to be a rural or urban village, lose out on the benefits of "Village's". I feel that if 50-75% of the land area outlined for a village is used for agriculture, horticulture & livestock, and fishing & aquaculture, the population cluster should be called a village, & should qualify as a village irrespective of the population size. The population of rural India is estimated to be 700 million.

Once the definition of a village is agreed upon, then adequate resources, means & ends should be provided to The Village Panchayat. All the land holdings should be consolidated as one farm and should be managed & farmed as one farm by the elected Panchayat. The entire land holding of the village should be partitioned as per soil quality, irrigation facilities, location, and size, and the farmland owners should be given equity in the overall cooperative to enjoy the kind & cash returns that will be earned by the "Village Farm" according to his/her equity share.

Empowering Village Panchayats with essential resources and infrastructure is a crucial step in fostering sustainable and self-reliant agricultural communities. Your comprehensive list addresses various aspects, ensuring a holistic approach to village development. Let's delve into the specifics:

1. Polycarbonate Greenhouses and Drip Irrigation: Introducing modern farming techniques promotes efficient resource use, controlled environments, and increased productivity.
2. Clean Water Supply: Access to clean water is fundamental for both agriculture and human consumption, contributing to overall health and well-being.
3. Sewage Systems: Implementing proper waste disposal systems is essential for maintaining environmental sustainability and hygiene in the village.
4. Mechanized Farm Equipment: Providing advanced agricultural machinery, including tractors, streamlines farming processes, making them more efficient and less labour-intensive.
5. Solar-Powered Equipment: Embracing solar technology for pumps, cookers, lights, coolers, and fans promotes sustainability and reduces reliance on conventional energy sources.

6. Warehousing Facilities: Adequate storage for agricultural produce ensures minimal wastage and better market access for farmers.
7. Organic Manure & Compost: Encouraging organic farming practices aligns with environmental sustainability and healthier agricultural produce.

Additional Points:

1. Employment Prioritization: Prioritizing landless laborers for farm-related employment ensures inclusive growth and supports the rural workforce.
2. Infrastructure & Connectivity: Robust hardware, software, and telecommunication facilities, coupled with high-speed internet, connect villages to national initiatives and markets.
3. Online Education System: Providing free education, including necessary resources, fosters knowledge and skills development, preparing the youth for diverse opportunities.
4. Family Planning: Promoting planned parenthood ensures responsible family growth and can contribute to improved socio-economic conditions. The emphasis on announcing plans and availing medical facilities encourages a proactive approach to family planning.
5. Transition to Educated Elderly: Gradually transitioning to an educated elderly workforce in Panchayats aligns with the changing landscape of rural governance. Leveraging the expertise of educated individuals in various fields ensures efficient management and decision-making.
6. Agro-Produce Logistics: Establishing a comprehensive agro-produce logistics department is

essential for streamlining the supply chain from farmers to consumers. Real-time price information through an app can empower farmers and enhance transparency in the market.

7. Shift to Drip Irrigation and Greenhouse Cropping: Encouraging the shift from water-intensive crops to more sustainable practices like drip irrigation and greenhouse cropping addresses environmental concerns and optimizes water usage.

36. From Emissions To No Emissions

Managing water resources is a critical global challenge, especially with a growing population and unpredictable precipitation patterns. Your proposal suggests the creation of an Indian National Water Pipeline Grid (INWPG) as a comprehensive solution. Let's refine and rephrase:

To address the pressing issue of water scarcity amidst a rising population and erratic rainfall patterns, I propose the establishment of the Indian National Water Pipeline Grid (INWPG). Detailed information about this initiative can be found on my website www.omdic.biz under the "Services I Offer" section, specifically the 5th Offering.

The fundamental concept revolves around deploying robust, large-diameter plastic pipes with a two-foot diameter across the country, forming a grid for water supply. These pipes will be color- coded based on the type of water and its designated usage. The color-coded system is as follows:

- Blue: Reserved for fresh water designated for human and animal consumption, as well as washing purposes.
- Green: Dedicated to agricultural water, including a mix with fertilizers and pesticides, aiming to enhance agricultural productivity.
- Yellow: Allocated for industrial water requirements.
- Red: Designated for polluted or dirty water from various sources. This water will undergo treatment and recycling processes, ultimately being reintroduced into the blue, green, and yellow water systems through respective pipelines.
- Orange: Targeted at pre-flood water management and control, integrated with strategic ground reservoirs. This proactive approach aims to dissipate and manage water in real-time, preventing flood scenarios by redirecting excess water into groundwater.

This comprehensive and color-coded system ensures efficient water distribution, recycling, and proactive flood management, contributing to sustainable water usage across various sectors.

The proposed plastic pipelines forming the Indian National Water Pipeline Grid (INWPG) are designed to optimize water distribution, efficiently managing areas with excess water and redirecting it to regions facing water scarcity. This innovative system will be overseen by independent mainframe computers and dedicated satellites, enabling real-time monitoring and dynamic adjustments based on weather forecasts. The plastic pipelines, with a diameter of two feet or less, will be strategically laid either above the ground, underground, or on the ground, enjoying the right of way.

To ensure continuous operation, solar pumps will power the pipelines during the day, supplemented by battery or electricity backup during the night. The entire length of the pipelines will be guarded by personnel, creating job opportunities across various regions and sectors.

Connecting these pipelines to Plastic Greenhouses equipped with plastic pipeline-based drip irrigation systems will facilitate the cultivation of diverse crops throughout the country. This approach offers a more efficient alternative to the River Connecting plan, avoiding issues such as water evaporation and the potential reduction of water flow to planned destinations caused by farms along connecting canals and rivers.

Furthermore, the INWPG aims to prevent the unnecessary flow of fresh river water into oceans and seas, subject to environmental conditions and circumstances. By optimizing water usage, this initiative ensures sustainable water management across diverse agricultural landscapes.

It is recommended to prioritize the focus on crude petroleum-based plastic, PVC, and polymer pipelines along with their grids. This strategic emphasis aims to repurpose crude petroleum capacities for zero-emission applications, particularly in the production of plastics, PVC, and polymers for pipeline grids. This transition would redirect crude petroleum capacities away from emission-heavy uses and towards environmentally friendly alternatives. The execution of such projects can be particularly advantageous in regions like the Middle East, where crude petroleum is abundant, and water shortages are prevalent.

The Integrated Network of Water Pipelines and Grids (INWPG) project, conceived in 2009, aligns with this vision. By utilizing heavy-duty plastics, it becomes possible to construct multi-story farms, offering increased agricultural space. For instance, a 4-story structure on a 1-acre plot can effectively provide farming space equivalent to 5 acres, catering to crops that predominantly grow underground. Additionally, the potential applications of these plastics extend to constructing greenhouses on both multi-story farms and traditional ground-level farms, complemented by plastic drip irrigation systems.

Moreover, the plastic produced could serve as an alternative to paper, meeting various paper- related requirements. This transformative approach allows crude petroleum utilization to shift from traditional refining processes (petrol, diesel, and kerosene) to the creation of durable plastic infrastructures. These innovations are poised to receive positive reception from environmental advocates and anti-plastic movements due to their extended shelf lives.

As the need for petrol and diesel pump stations diminishes, a proposed solution involves converting these stations into battery charging stations. These revamped stations can cater to two and three-wheeler electric vehicles and support fruit and vegetable retailers, sourced from the INWPG Plastic Farms. The refrigeration requirements for these products can be met through solar systems during the day and, when necessary, by battery or electricity during the night. This multifaceted approach not only addresses environmental concerns but also capitalizes on the evolving landscape of sustainable energy and transportation.

37. Recommendations On Central Bank Digital Currency (Cbdc)

The recent news reveals that the Reserve Bank of India (RBI) has initiated a pilot project for Central Bank Digital Currency (CBDC), focusing on intra-bank transaction settlements involving nine banks in India. This groundbreaking step is anticipated to extend to real-time learning experiences in retail transactions for Micro, Small, and Medium Enterprises (MSMEs), with a potential commencement date as early as the end of November 2022, as reported by NDTV. However, the Planned and Organized Deficit Spending (PODS) book research team offers the following recommendations for the CBDC e-digital currency:

1. Digital vs Cash Transactions: To enhance the acceptance of CBDC, which currently competes with cash transactions, there is a need to incentivize digital transactions. The research team suggests tying every unit of digital currency issuance to a corresponding physical supply of goods, services, or agricultural products. This responsible issuance

strategy is expected to act as a safeguard against inflation.

2. Responsible Issuance: The principle of responsible issuance emphasizes that until there is a matching supply of goods or services for every unit of digital currency issued, continuous digital issuance can take place. This approach ensures a balanced demand-supply distribution of digital currency, eliminating the need for traditional economic concepts such as the velocity of money or the multiplier of money.

Money multiplier effect

Speed of Digital Transactions:

- It is argued that tools like Cash Reserve Ratio (CRR), Statutory Liquidity Ratio (SLR), Repo Rate, and Reverse Repo Rate are not effective in the digital realm due to the near-instantaneous nature of digital transactions. This could be allowed in case supply can catch up with the multiplier and velocity numbers. CRR & SLR are not relevant.
- This rapid circulation may indeed pose challenges for traditional monetary policy tools that rely on time lags to influence economic conditions. However, capacities can be planned to be flexible and in line with population & employment growth.

Digital Currency and Overnight Lending:

- You suggest that digital currency could nullify overnight lending, as central banks can issue digital

money instantly, eliminating the need for overnight borrowing.
- The ability to issue digital currency on-demand could potentially reshape the dynamics of interbank lending.

Zero Percent Loans and Lending Rates:

- The idea is presented that loans could be issued at zero percent, covering the cost of digital infrastructure for issuing digital currency.
- After recovering these costs, lending rates could approach zero, encouraging more borrowing.

Unidirectional Conversion and 100% Guarantee:

- I propose a one-way conversion from cash to digital currency, with all deposits in digital currency being 100% guaranteed subject to the conditions mentioned earlier.
- The aim is to ensure the stability and reliability of digital currency, possibly addressing concerns about its acceptance.

Restrictions on Use and Taxation:

- I suggest that digital currency should only be spent or utilized digitally, not for speculative purposes.
- Interest in digital deposits could be higher than that on cash deposits, incentivizing digital adoption. Cash is dead and not King. CBDC reigns.
- Profits from digital transactions could be subject to lower tax rates to encourage their use.

Prevention of a Run-on Digital Currency:

- I highlight that a run-on digital currency in banks is not possible, possibly due to the guaranteed nature of digital deposits.
- It's important to note that the implementation of such a system would involve various complexities, regulatory considerations, and potential unintended consequences. Digital currencies, their regulation, and their impact on monetary policy are topics of ongoing discussion and exploration by central banks around the world.

Centralized Control by the Central Bank (RBI):

- All digital currency issuance must be approved and sanctioned by the central bank (RBI).
- Digital money accounts and loans would be directly connected to the central bank to manage inflationary or deflationary impacts at a branch level.

Velocity and Multiplier Effects:

- Digital currency adoption is proposed to control velocity and multiplier effects, eliminating the need for these effects seen in cash and cheque transactions.
- The shift to digital currency is considered a strategy to reduce inflationary pressures.

Zero Taxation and Transparent Transactions:

- The move to digital currency aims for transparent transactions, potentially leading to zero taxation.

- All business transactions would be recorded in digital banking infrastructure to minimize hidden economic activities.

Money Supply and Inflation Dynamics:

- For every unit of digital currency issued, there is a one-to-one relationship with physical supply, contrasting with the multiplier effect in cash transactions.
- Controlled issuance of digital currency is proposed as a mechanism to nullify inflationary or deflationary effects.

Example of Economic Impact:

- An example is provided where digital currency, issued as an interest-free loan to a producer, stimulates production, consumption, and creates a self-sustaining economic cycle.

Role of Saving and Taxation:

- Savings and taxation are identified as potential sources of inflationary or deflationary impact due to leakages in demand-supply pipelines.
- Proposed measures include keeping savings in digital mode, creating interest rates digitally, and ensuring spending on non-inflationary goods and services.

Control of Inflation through Digital Money Issuance:

- To control inflation, the proposal suggests issuing digital money to existing capacities contributing to inflation, with the ability to address short-term capacity gaps through imports using digital currency.
- The PODS CBDC OM-0 HQ will be in Delhi, India.

Discouraging Foreign Direct Investments (FDI):

- The proposal suggests discouraging FDI due to the potential impact on the domestic currency.
- Example: When Vedanta Resources raises $20 billion, it leads to the issuance of approximately 1660 billion rupees, affecting global inflation.

Taxing NRIs and PIOs for Hard Currency Requirements:

- Non-Resident Indians (NRIs) and People of Indian Origins (PIOs) could be taxed to meet hard currency requirements.
- Taxing 30 million individuals with a USD 4000 tax could yield $120 billion annually besides inward remittances.
- This foreign exchange can be immediately credited to payers in the form of digital currency onshore accounts in India, with no questions asked and attract a tax free 13% interest per annum with the CBDC account being 100% guaranteed.

Foreign Exchange for Critical Imports:

- The $120 billion generated through taxation is deemed sufficient for critical imports in India.

- Proposes agreements with importing countries for payments in digital rupees only.

Zero Interest Rate Lines of Credit for Make in India Scheme:

- Recommends offering zero interest rate-bearing lines of credit in INR to foreign companies contributing to the Make in India scheme.

Digital Currency Issuance by the Government:

- Argues that the government doesn't need to issue interest-yielding bonds when it can digitally issue money backed by the supply of physical goods.
- Advises against issuing sovereign debt in foreign currencies, suggesting the government can digitally create money as needed.

Introduction of E-Digital Currency (OM):

- Recommends naming the e-digital currency for India as "OM" with the symbol "0."
- Proposes parallel transactions using both INR and OM simultaneously in the beginning.

Note: with OM and its symbol zero one would transact in zero meaning one would receive zero and one would give zero. Please note that this currency, to work, can only be issued in Bharath or as one global currency. A global currency is possible if it is issued by a domestic CBDC with the condition that every economy runs at zero state meaning that the economy is fully saturated in due course without inflation or deflation and produces no surpluses unless these products are intentionally and transparently made, perhaps because of circumstances that are unique to that request surplus CBDC economy. This is not about a religion or Hindus because besides being the oldest religion it is a philosophy that lets you choose your own religion without physical or mental force and can be practiced privately with oneself.

These recommendations suggest a shift toward a more digitally oriented and self-reliant economic approach for India and other countries, with an emphasis on leveraging digital currency, taxation, and foreign exchange management to meet economic goals. The suggestions align with the concept of reducing reliance on traditional financial instruments in favour of more direct and digitally facilitated economic strategies.

Lastly, profit leads to inflation. This is so when an apple costing 125/- units of CBDC to grow and reach the customer from the farmer is sold to the actual farmer for 200/- units of CBDC. Do you see the extra 75/- units of CBDC putting an inflation impact on apples. It's still capitalism (maximizing profit) but the other side of the coin is maximizing deficits. Not Gross Domestic Product but Gross Deficit Products. Even better, as Dr. Narayan Murthy put it: "Compassionate Capitalism."

Abbreviations

AI- Artificial Intelligence

BTT- Banking Transaction Tax CPM- Critical Path Method

DEADS – Distributed Equilibrium Allowable Deficit Spending DM- Demand Monitor

DM- Digital Mint DM- Digital Mint

EAC – Economic Administrative Committee EC- Economic Coordinator

EFT- Economic failure tax EME- Eleven market economy ETME- Eight market economy FDI- Foreign Direct Investment GOI- Government of India

HQ- Headquarters

IGB- Indian Global Bank

IGCB- Indian Global Changeover Bank ILC- Industry Life Cycles

L1- Lowest priced bid

LIBOR – London Interbank Offer Rate LLM- Large Language Models

LME- Latest Model Market Economy LOOP- Law of One Price

LTT- Learning and teaching tour ML-Machine Learning

MMT- Modern Monetary Theory MOF- Ministry of Finance

MRP- Maximum Retail Price

MSAEMM- Mercedes School of Automobile, Engineering, Management, and Marketing MSIAEM- Maruti Suzuki Institute of Automobile Engineering and Management

MSP- Minimum Support Price NN- Natural Needs

NPA- Non-Performing Assets NRI- Non-Resident Indian OVF- One Village Farm

PCGDB- PODS CBDC Global Domestic Bank PCGIB-PODS CBDC Global International Bank PLI- Production Linked Incentives

PODS – Planned and Organized Deficit Spending PPPP-Purchasing Power Parity Price

PURR- Product Usage Responsibility Regulations QQE-Quality, quantity and employment

S.E.B- State Electricity Board SEZ- Special Economic Zone SM- Supply Monitor

SSS- Sustainable, Saturated Supply T1- Best technology bid

TME- Ten Market Economy

UID- Unique Identification Numbers WPI- Wholesale Price Index

Bibliography

Bharat-Ram, V., 2017 Evolution of Economic Ideas- ADAM SMITH TO AMARTYA SEN and beyond. Published in India by Oxford University Press.

Deming, W.E., 2000. The new economics: for industry, government, education. MIT Press. Cambridge, Mass.

Engelhardt, Lucas M. Modern Monetary Theory, Recorded at the Mises Institute in Auburn, Alabama on 19 July, 2019.

Forbes, S., Lewis, N. and Ames, E., 2022. Inflation: What it Is, why It's Bad, and how to Fix it. Encounter Books.

Kelton, Stephanie A. The Deficit Myth book published on June 9, 2020 and is a New York Times bestseller.

Kelton, Stephanie A. How MMT can help us understand the economy? You Tube Bloomberg Markets & Finance published via a video on Oct 7, 2019. 42000 Views.

Kelton, Stephanie A. Presidential Lecture Series- How will we pay for it? Making public money work for us- at Stony Brooks University, Staller Center Main Stage, 100 Nicolls

Road, NY 11794 New York at 4 PM ET on Monday, 15 October, 2018.

Mitchell, Bill. De-mystifying Modern Monetary Theory: By Institute for New Economic Thinking, Published on You Tube on 12/28/2014. 122,000 plus views.

Mitchell, Bill. Mosler, Warren & Watts, Martin. Macroeconomics by The Gower Initiative for Modern Monetary Studies, Birmingham on 11 May 2019. Published on YouTube on 20 May 2019. 12,000 +views.

Planned & Organized Deficit Spending (PODS) by Vidur Sahgal, 2023.

Ritenour, Shawn. Austrian Economics versus Keynesian Macroeconomics and Modern Monetary Theory, YouTube on 15 July, 2020 by Misesmedia 9000+ views.

Skousen, Mark. The Big Three in Economics- Adam Smith, Karl Marx & John Maynard Keynes, published by Thrift Books in 2015. Narrated by Jeff Riggenbach.

Wapshott, Nicholas. Samuelson Friedman: The Battle of the Free Market, published by W.W.Norton & Company & released on 10 November 2020. Narrated by Chris MacDonnell.

Wray Randall L. Everything you want to know about MMT, Bloomberg Markets & Finance, Youtube video, Bard College 26 July 2020

Wray Randall L. Modern Monetary Theory for beginners, St. Francis College published on YouTube video on 4/25/2018.

Printed in the USA
CPSIA information can be obtained
at www.ICGtesting.com
LVHW072140120424
777208LV00006B/143
* 9 7 9 8 8 9 3 8 3 0 5 6 9 *